DEDICATION

To my beloved dog Raider.

The tragedy of losing you was the catalyst to begin a new life.

Your sacrifice saved my life.

BROKEN
IS A CHOICE

My Resurrection from Trauma and Shame

Jennifer,
Thank you for your support.
Love and blessings!
♡ Kelly Staib

KELLY STAIB

Printed in the United States of America

ISBN: 978-1-952756-51-1

For details email joan@victoriousyoupress.com
or visit us at www.victoriousyoupress.com

ACKNOWLEDGEMENTS

Terri––You planted the first seed of sobriety for me years before I did anything. The attraction rather than promotion left me wanting what you had. Thank you for answering the phone when I was ready for help.

Jen––You helped me become the woman God created me to be. You showed me the ugly side I wanted to be rid of. You showed me how to live life through a new pair of lenses. Your gentle but direct nature was exactly what I needed. I am forever grateful for your friendship and spiritual influence.

Dave––When I thought of the perfect man for me, God exceeded my heart's desires and gave me you. Everything about you and the man you are amazes me. I thank God for you and our life we are building together. Your support of my recovery and growth means the world to me. Thank you for your encouragement, warm embraces, and pointing out to me when I go sideways that it is time to get my butt to a meeting.

Thank you to my friends who encouraged me to share my story. Especially Jeff, who was the thorn in my side and nagged me until I started writing.

CONTENTS

INTRODUCTION

D o you justify your actions and your decisions? Do you fight to remain the same? Do you want others to change? Does chaos and drama surround you? Do you secretly wish you did not do things just to please others? Do you have unhealthy coping skills? If you answer "Yes" to any of these questions, then you can relate to something I experienced. I have found a solution.

At thirty-two years of age, I took my first breath. Not literally of course, but that is what it seemed like starting a new life again. From age fourteen to thirty-two, there was an eighteen-year time warp. Like being in a coma. I aged but lacked all normal development that would have taken place in those years. Everything I thought I knew and learned from fourteen on seemed to be wrong and led me into a deep hole.

When I quit drinking and surrendered to change, I learned to breathe again. I needed and finally found a better way to be myself. I learned life from a new perspective, rebuilt a lot of it from scratch, and have transformed along the way. This discovery was something so foreign to the path I was on for half of my life.

What did I discover? The intimacy, acceptance, and love I desired from people for so many years I found in a relationship with Jesus Christ. I did not know my decision to follow Him and get sober would change my world and give me a life beyond my wildest imagination.

Although this book is my story, my experiences and lessons learned reflect the lives of so many people who suffer from addictions and destructive patterns. There is hope because I live in the solution to a new life. Believe it or not, I would change *nothing* about my past because I know it had to happen to get me where I am today.

REMAINING BROKEN WAS MY CHOICE.

I believe everything we do in life is a choice, and remaining broken is one of those choices. I remained broken for close to twenty years, until I found a solution. It may sound easy, but change is often difficult. It took time and a lot of action on my part to get to a place of peace and freedom. My life was shattered and in turmoil before I started the journey of recovery that is so indescribable only a person in this place can understand. Thankfully, new life is possible for anyone who wants to change.

Sexual abuse, mental abuse, abandonment, an eating disorder, and shame are what I experienced in my life. I used alcohol, drugs, self-harm, and people pleasing to cope and hide the pain. All these hurdles I have struggled with during my life. These challenges do not define who I am but what I have overcome by the grace of God.

Quitting drinking was the catalyst that gave me a starting point of where recovery began. I did not know that once I quit drinking, the journey really began. Alcohol was only a symptom of the problem––and the problem was me. Once I put the bottle down and started a life-long program, my world turned around. My feelings of abandonment, unworthiness, fear, insecurity, abuse, shame, and rejection kept me stuck for many years. I have now recreated a life free from shame and condemnation.

Hearing someone say, "I am an alcoholic" is not something you hear often or ever unless it's in a movie or recovery meeting. Introducing myself as an alcoholic or person in recovery was scary and shameful at first. It is not like that any longer, and I am grateful to admit, "I am an alcoholic and in recovery." Admitting that fact was the beginning of a beautiful story of transformation. Some people consider the term alcoholic a negative label, but I respectfully disagree. Acknowledging it saved my life because I started a priceless journey of transformation.

As I spent six months writing and reflecting, I uncovered many suppressed memories. My stories reveal how chaotic and dramatic the life of an addicted person can be. The new me is quite the bubbly and fun-loving person, and it's all a natural high. Today, I am proud of who I am and of my life.

There was so much more than just quitting alcohol that I uncovered and needed to heal from. I recovered from a life filled with trauma that took me to rock bottom and did not reveal itself until I worked on myself. If I could work my recovery as hard as I worked my addiction, there was hope for me. I found my purpose in life, and it is to share my story of recovery, the effort I put forth daily, and the hope there is for others. It is an ongoing journey every single day, but changing was much easier than remaining the same. My old life was a nightmare.

In these years of discovery and change, I have been a busy lady and taken massive action. Was it easy? Absolutely not. It was dreadfully painful, and I shed a lot of tears. I think I cried every day for over a year. I did not know how to change, and I feared the unknown. There was grieving everything that I was losing and broke up with the longest relationship I had from age fourteen to thirty-two...alcohol. My marriage, beloved dogs, family, and friends were left behind. I cried from uncertainty of the future and the overwhelming emotions I experienced sober for the first time. I had to feel the feelings, and that was tough for someone who drank to erase any negative feelings. It seemed like anytime I met someone new and they asked me about myself, I could not hold back the tears. I was so ashamed of myself and the person I had been all those years.

Was all this work worth it? Looking back, you better believe it was! There was a lot of pain and tears, but that is part of the healing process. God surely showed up every day and guided me because I took the effort to invite Him in to my life. Did I fall short and make mistakes? I certainly did, and sometimes the same ones over and over. I still make mistakes, and that is okay.

Did I get into recovery right away? Not really. I quit drinking, but there were other habits that I replaced alcohol with that were unhealthy. I did not start out winning at life but by making mistakes and learning from them. Instead, I failed miserably over and over until I tired of making them and learned how to quit. I discovered that failure is just feedback for the next time, and you cannot really fail unless you stop trying. So, do not stop trying!

I began recovery from my addictive life and am determined to continue it until the day God calls me home. There is a quote that is often used in recovery meetings that says, "Sobriety is never owned. It is rented. And rent is due every day." Recovery is a journey that you do not graduate from, but it is an event in life to celebrate. Personal growth needs to be a lifetime commitment because addictions can start up again by a bad choice at the next opportunity.

I learned that once God reveals an issue for me to work on and I grow through it, another one is revealed. As a sinful and imperfect person, I will always have something to work on. The blessing and joy are knowing and celebrating the progress I've made from the person I used to be. I have the choice to resist what God wants for me and risk falling back into addiction. If I am open to receive His opportunity for growth and loving hand to help me through, it eventually always presents itself. There is a quote from the *Tao Te Ching* text of Chinese philosophy that says, "When the student is ready, the teacher will appear."

When I was in early sobriety, I wanted to read how to fix myself. I was broken, damaged goods. There was something wrong with me, and there had to be a book out there to repair me. I was not prepared for anything I encountered in life and royally screwed up my twenties and early thirties. My thinking was not healthy and even worse was my relationship with others. I thought, *There must be books out there that can show me how not to be such a broken person!* My desire was to learn how to make better choices and why I behaved in certain ways. I often asked myself, *Why am I so selfish? Why don't I know better? Why do I feel alone and unloved? What keeps me stuck in toxic relationships? Why do I seek approval from people who don't seem to care about me?*

Have you ever asked yourself these questions? Do you know somebody who does? My hope is that my experiences and what I have learned on this journey will inspire others, let them know there is help no matter how bad the addiction, and the first step is making the choice to change.

There is a lot of shame in my story, and you may ask, "Kelly, why disclose all this personal, humiliating information?" I am my authentic self, and this is my truth journey. I choose to be vulnerable and share the unflattering stories about my family, relationships, and life experience. When one person shows their vulnerability and authenticity with others, including the lows and depths of despair, God can use that in amazing ways. When we share with someone how we overcame our struggle, we give hope to that person. Hope is sometimes all we need to continue to take the first step, and then the next, and the next. Hope is grasping for a positive future. I am grateful to the person who created the acronym H.O.P.E. that stands for **Hold On Pain Ends.**

A pastor I listen to says, "God calls people according to their potential." A few years ago, God put writing my story on my heart. I have had many internal battles with doubt and indecision about putting it all out there, but I trust God will use this book for His glory. What prevented me from writing it for so long was my struggle with seeking the approval of people. I imagined them making comments like, "Who does Kelly think she is writing a book? She has no business doing that." "What can she offer? She was just a drunk mess." "Who will read her book? She has nothing worth writing about." There are people who did not want me to share about my life because it could implicate them and their part in my story. I had one person say, "You know that telling the truth could really hurt someone." Seeking approval from people that are not on my growth journey does not have a place in my life today, and that is okay. The more I grow, the more people that are not meant to be in my life will fall away.

God knows there are things in my story and experience I have overcome that will resonate with others. It is not about me, anyway. The message is for others to know you do not have to remain in pain any longer. You can heal and move forward, escaping from the chains that keep you stuck in a prison.

I am in the business of effort, and God is in the business of results. I plant seeds and God sows them. The Bible says, "It is not important who does the planting, or who does the watering. What is important is that God makes the seed grow" (1 Corinthians 3:7 NLT). My desire for you is that as you read the stories, consider my advice, ponder the scriptures, and feel encouraged to know you are not alone on your journey and there is a great plan for your life!

PART ONE

THE TRAUMATIZING
YOUNGER YEARS

ALONE AND AFRAID

I had a therapist once tell me that my early memories of being lost and scared followed me throughout my entire life until I decided to get help. She said, "No wonder you've had traumatic experiences. Nobody protected you from abuse like you should have been. You had an unstable upbringing and not given what you needed to develop properly as a teenager and adult."

I had many early memories of being a child between three and five, and none of them were positive. They were of being afraid and in some sort of neglected situation. I remember being lost in a store when I was about three. I felt alone and panic for the first time. That feeling came back often in my youth.

My earliest memory of molestation was at two different babysitter's houses between the ages of three and five. The first time was in Virginia when I was about three. I was napping and an older boy came into my room and pulled my underwear down. There was a bowl of pot-pourri on the bedstand, and he took a few of the small white flower buds and rubbed me down there with them. I froze and did not say a word. I just laid there and pretended to be asleep. I did not understand what was going on, but it didn't seem right.

The second time was in West Virginia when I was about five. I was sitting on the babysitter's husband's lap watching a TV show. His fingers touched me under my dress and then slid inside my underwear. I just sat there frozen again, not knowing what to do. I didn't tell anyone.

When I was twelve, a relative came into my room in the morning as I woke up. I just laid there, trying not to move. I was uncomfortable and frightened about what might happen in the next few minutes. He kneeled on the floor next to me and put his hands under the sheets. He rubbed his hands around my underwear like the others had done and then went inside it. Again, I did nothing but lay there and freeze. I didn't tell anyone, but knew it was wrong.

During those three situations, no one said anything to me. They took their own liberty with my innocent body and then left the room. This happened again and again until in my mid-thirties. I finally had enough and learned that I could say no and push men off of me. That was a lot of years of freezing and allowing others to use me for their own pleasure.

Despite the trauma of being molested, I have some wonderful memories of growing up in West Virginia. There were many kids my age to play with, and we had fun. I was free to roam the neighborhood in the late 80s and early 90s because that was life back then. We left the house on our bikes to go meet up with the other neighborhood kids. We stayed out all day and went home when it was time for dinner.

Unfortunately, my good memories are overshadowed by the bad ones. When I was ten years old, there were two boys in the neighborhood who I went over to play with at their houses. While in their rooms, they shut the door and exposed themselves to me. I screamed and pushed my way out. I had no idea what they were thinking, but I was there to play, and they had other ideas in mind. Once again, I did not tell anyone. These experiences added to my feelings of fear and being alone.

My parents divorced when I was less than a year old. My mother later told me, "I divorced your dad because he is an alcoholic and physically abused me." She had nothing good to say about him my entire childhood, and all I knew was what she told me. "He is a no-good piece of crap who abused me and drug me across the street by my hair when I was pregnant with you." I have no memories of my biological parents together. I never saw my dad drunk when I was with him, but I was frightened one time when I was about five. He was speeding and driving erratically with me in the car, and I remember praying, "Dear God, please get Daddy and me there safely."

Mom remarried when I was five, and they acted like what I thought was normal. I have positive memories of the early years of holidays and birthdays, but that is mainly because of the pictures I saved from them. My mom and step-dad had only a couple of fights that I saw. Mom was typically the instigator, from my perspective, and she got physical and verbally abusive. Some words that came out of her mouth were awful. She told me when we were alone that she wished he were different. Mom was never satisfied with him and complained to me often about him. As I got older, I picked up this "never satisfied" mentality.

I spent every other weekend with my biological father per the custody arrangement. He had a birthday party for me when I was five and bought me one of those small plastic pools. I was playing and laughing when my brother, Jimmy, who is two years older, held my head under the water. I was frightened and struggled to get away, gasping for air as I came up. When I started crying, Jimmy just laughed. That ended my fun time in the pool. Another fearful memory added to so many.

My dad also remarried, and I considered her a monster. Later that day at my pool party, I was in my bedroom alone. My stepmother came in and knelt beside me. I vividly remember her saying, "There are monsters in your closet that are going to get you! I don't know why you come here. Your father doesn't love you." She clearly had some issues of her own to say that to a child. I went home and told my mother. She called my dad, they argued, and Mom hung up on him. I never saw my stepmother again after that weekend and will never forget how terrified I felt that day.

My father's marriage to her ended not long after that. I do not know the real reason and he never shared with me. Dad and I were not close when I was growing up, and I never thought to ask. I only heard bits and pieces from Mom that she acquired from the second wife. My perception over the years is they had a party lifestyle, and the alcohol and abuse were too much for her and she left. If there was a different truth, I will never know.

Dad was nice to me when I saw him, but it was a rare occasion when I did. It was only on Easter, Thanksgiving, and Christmas from the time I was five through high school. He always seemed like he did not want me around or that I was a burden. The encounters felt awkward, and we were strangers to each other. I wondered why he did not want to see me more or fight my mom to get me on the weekends after the second wife left. I felt rejected by Dad and unloved. Jimmy still went to stay with him every other weekend and eventually moved in when my mom found him too much to handle.

When I was seventeen, Dad and I made plans to go horseback riding. I think this may have been the only time he and I ever did anything with just the two of us. I was very excited to spend time with him. We ran into a friend of his that he introduced to me as "Someone I have known for twenty years." The man said, "I did not know you had a daughter." I thought, *Really? Am I not good enough to even talk about?* I felt deeply hurt, and it lingered that day that had started out special. I don't remember Dad saying anything about the comment and never forgot how it made me feel--so alone and unloved.

ROLLER COASTER

In one therapy session I had while writing this book, I walked through as many details as I could remember of what it was like growing up with my mother. I told the therapist, "It was like a roller coaster ride with lots of up and downs. My mom was really high or really low." Sharing this out loud and slowly remembering what happened was painful and emotional. I said, "I never knew what each day would look like. I checked Mom's mood to determine how I thought the day or events would go. We could be having a good day, then something happened and she snapped. I don't remember normal family days at all. The only memories that come to mind are either fun or awful. That was my normal."

The highs with Mom were her telling me how much she loved me and giving me hugs and kisses. I loved our shopping days and drive-thru fast-food stops. Sometimes she kept me out of school to go shopping. Mom loved to take pictures of me and play dress up. She entered me in school pageants, and it was always fun to wear pretty dresses. My mom's love language was gift giving, and she loved to spend money. Gift giving is also one of my love languages. Mom would say, "If your brother behaved like you do, he would get this treatment, too." It made me happy that I pleased her.

Mother had a tough time raising my brother. She said Jimmy had behavioral issues, and she took him to a psychologist.

He refused to take any of the prescribed medication. There was always yelling, flipping furniture over, and breaking things when he did not listen to her or did something she did not approve of. When he became a teenager, Jimmy went to live with Dad.

The lows with Mom unfortunately outweighed the highs. There was yelling, physical and verbal abuse, isolation, lots of crying, depression, and suicide threats. The more I talk out loud about her and her behaviors, I'm sure she had mental health issues but did nothing more than take an antidepressant. It seemed over the years the antidepressants did not work, or she stopped taking them. I do not recall her going to a counselor, therapist, or getting any help in general. You would think that after I told my mother about the sexual abuse I experienced, she would put me in counseling. She was more concerned with how the relative who molested me could do that to *her*, rather than how it affected *me*.

My mother and stepfather divorced when I was thirteen. That was when I started to experience emotional neglect from Mom. She and I lived alone until I moved out at eighteen to go to college. I needed a mother to guide me, give me boundaries and direction, and life skills. There was none of that. I had a barely present mother who doted on me in front of others and neglected my emotional needs when no one was around. I loved the attention and praise she gave me, but the actions never seemed to match her words.

I witnessed the relationships Mom had with the men she dated. It was a revolving door of the next perfect guy she put on a pedestal. She always met them at the bar while she was out with friends. Sometimes she brought them home and introduced them to me. Some were okay and nice, and some creeped me out. One guy hit on me when she was not around. I felt very uncomfortable but didn't tell her. There were so many feelings and experiences I kept to myself. I later discovered why and got the help and healing I needed.

My mother had extended periods of depression. One day, she came home and had quit her job at the doctor's office. It seemed she was in bed for months after that. Mom did not have a boyfriend at the time because when there was a man around, she bounced around the house high on life. I came home from high school one day to get ready for a cheerleading banquet. Mother was still in bed depressed after several weeks. I asked, "Are you going to come with me like you promised?" She scowled at me and said, "No. Just leave me alone!" I left her room in tears.

I hated being the only one at these functions with no parents. I felt rejected, unloved, and alone. This made my anxiety worse. I experienced my first ulcer at fifteen from all the anxiety I kept inside me and did not know it was anxiety until years later when I got help. I feared everyone looked at me and talked about me saying, "Where is her mother?" My mother had issues, but I did not understand why she stopped participating in what was important to me and was rarely at my sporting events. It was sad to watch and experience Mom's depression. I felt angry and resented her because she did nothing to help herself.

My friend Jade's parents were kind to me, and they seemed to enjoy having me around. I think they sensed I felt rejected and alone because they treated me like one of their kids. They asked questions about school and "How was your day?" I loved spending the night at my friends' houses, preferred it over mine, but they rarely stayed over with me.

I have many memories of Mom making suicide threats in front of me. She would say, "I should just blow my brains out" in a fit of rage or like it was a normal part in a conversation. There were outbursts screaming, "I want to die!" and me crying and begging her to stop. I probably heard her say over a hundred times, "I just want to die. I hate my life and wish God would take me out." She said it a few times while I wrote this book. Mother still won't get the help she needs.

It was terribly hard for me to experience that trauma year after year and difficult to block it out of my memory. A few times, Mom drove me in the car and threatened to run into a telephone pole or tree. She would yell, "I want it to be over! All I have to do is turn the car into the tree, and it will all be over." I saw her bang her head on the steering wheel and wall, and she hit her head with her fists. I did a lot of crying and begging, and it was traumatic and exhausting to go through this experience. If I ever brought any of this up to her, she denied it and claimed no memory of it. I reminded her years later about some of these instances, and she told me, "You're crazy! How can you make up things like this?" It was all very confusing. Sometimes I thought, *Am I the one that is crazy?*

My mother disappeared at times, leaving others and me worried about her. Once in high school she made threats to kill herself and then left and turned off her phone so she could not be tracked or contacted. I was worried, scared, and left alone to take care of myself. She showed up a couple days later like nothing happened and expected me to continue with life. Mom took me shopping to make up for it, told me how much she loved me, and hugged and kissed me to make it better. But deep inside me, the pain got worse and nothing changed.

At an early age, I learned from my mother about comparison. I wanted to do what she did. I signed up for my first gym membership with Mom at thirteen. In high school I opted for four years of weightlifting instead of gym class. Mom had been a cheerleader, so I wanted to be a cheerleader. She was a skinny teenager, around 100 pounds, and condescendingly said, "I weighed less than you at your age" as she poked at my stomach or legs. Even when she said, "You're strong because you lift weights" I took it negatively that I should lose weight.

I started to obsess about my weight when I was fourteen. We lived beside the high school, and the track was on the other side of my fence. I ran around the track and then came home and weighed myself. For several years I was scale obsessed and focused on a number every day and when I could exercise next. Even though I was small, I compared myself to other girls all the time and always saw ones smaller than me. My mother was on many fad diets, so I repeated what I saw her do. I often ate as little as possible and was still not satisfied with myself. I knew little about health and nutrition or that a pound of muscle took up less space than a pound of fat. So, I looked at the pounds on the scale rather than the benefit of muscles.

Over time, I developed *body dysmorphia*, a mental health disorder that focuses on appearance and body image. I did not eat for many hours, then binge eat and throw up afterwards. As a teenager I felt anxious and didn't know what was wrong. I suffered from body dysmorphia for years, and it contributed to alcohol use as I got older. It took a miracle in my thirties to save me.

PART TWO

MAKING CHOICES
ON MY OWN

MY ADDICTION BEGINS

Since my mother was off in her own world not paying much attention to me, I started hanging with a different crowd. I was an athlete and played sports from the time I was seven. My friends were the cheerleaders and track kids from sports. When I got my driver's license at sixteen, I quit cheerleading and track. I had worked part time since I was thirteen. My first job was at my friend's mom's video store, then as a server at the neighborhood diner. I worked at a fast-food place, grocery store, bank, and as a server at a truck stop. I was good and made big tips.

I started liking boys when I was fourteen and had a couple of crushes that did not last very long. Hanging out with these teenage boys, I started drinking and smoking pot. I dated my first boyfriend the last two years of high school. He sold drugs, and I went with him to meet people to buy from or sell to. I thought I was cool being a drug dealer's girlfriend, probably because the people I hung out with seemed cool. What difference did being cool make? Even with a crowd, I still felt alone and rejected.

I drank and smoked as much as I could on the weekends. I became a daily cigarette smoker at fifteen. My friends started to change, and I hung out with an older crowd and not the girls who had been my long-time closest friends. I skipped school one time, but the fear of getting caught and in trouble was enough to make me stop. I was afraid of my mother's harsh punishment and scared of her. When I came home one time with alcohol on my breath, she punched me in the face. Once I smelled like cigarettes, and Mom pushed me down a flight of stairs. From then on, I hid the smell with perfume and mints. I lied often about my drinking and always minimized it. I would say, "I am the designated driver," so she felt more comfortable with me not coming home and staying out all night with friends.

I loved the way alcohol made me feel. It dulled my emotions and pain, and I felt great. I chased that feeling as often as I could, not realizing I was in denial of how I really felt about my life. I masked the pain for the next sixteen years and began a toxic relationship that I loved with alcohol.

HEADED TO COLLEGE

I wanted to get away from home and go to a university college. It was a battle because my mom wanted me to stay home and attend a community college. I believed she did not want me to succeed in life so she could feel superior. When I did anything to progress forward, Mom said in a condescending tone, "Good for you." She refocused the attention on her and told stories of what she was like at my age and what she did well.

I went away to West Virginia University and had hurdles to get in. Never receiving guidance about college prep, I entered my application late and was on academic probation the first semester. I felt Mom resented me going away to college because she only visited me twice in five years. She dropped me off, visited once my sophomore year, and came to my graduation. I was very insecure and felt like an inconvenience to her.

As the years went by, I became more like my mother and our relationship very dysfunctional. I never learned until years into my recovery the extent of our disorder. I was headed for trouble.

EATING DISORDER

Early in my freshman year of college, I was a size zero-to-two and determined not to gain the "freshman fifteen." It was extremely hard because I went out to the bars and house parties multiple times a week. We did late-night eating on the way back to the dorms. I was exercising every chance I could, but then it started to interfere with my social life and going to the bars.

I made the dangerous decision to force myself to throw up after meals. I felt like I was in control of my weight, a delusion that lasted for months. Then my roommate caught me purging in the community bathroom. I will never forget how she called me out in front of others on our floor, and I felt so embarrassed and humiliated. Praise God her actions and my own to quit were all it took to stop my bulimia eating disorder.

Unfortunately, my abnormal preoccupation with weight continued. I upped my working out and cardio and went to the gym two hours a day and sometimes twice in the same day. I started taking diet pills regularly and counted calories for the next several years. I ate fewer food calories so I could have more drink calories. I was obsessed with the gym and unhealthy dieting throughout my alcoholic relationship.

When I went home for the holidays, I stayed with friends and their family. My visit with my mom was always brief. I seemed to dread going to see her, but knew it was the right thing to do and thought something might change. I hoped it would be a pleasant visit, and sometimes it was, but usually not.

I never analyzed the anxiety I experienced around my mom until a couple of years after I got sober. I called her and initiated the visits. She always expected me to come to her, and I felt like an afterthought—unimportant and neglected. One time, I came home for Christmas break, and a group of friends and their parents––who were friends with my mom––all partied together. I got blackout drunk––not remembering anything I did or said––and apparently told my mom how I felt about her. I imagine it was harsh. The next day, Mom made comments like, "How dare you say those things to me? You are a hateful person." I just brushed it under the rug like she was nothing and continued my life. Wonder who I learned that from?

I was rude and disrespectful to my mother for the next ten years. I acted superior and treated her like crap. She was a neglectful mother, and I kept returning and acting mean––but always seemed to say, "I love you, Mom." This dysfunctional relationship was our normal life.

NO DIRECTION

When I entered college, I did not know what I wanted to do with my life. With an unsupportive home life, poor grades, a party attitude, and my drinking problem, there was a constant struggle to find a major and stick with it. I was also a bartender and waitress throughout college. Any money left after tuition, rent, and food was spent on alcohol and drugs.

I changed my major five times in college. I started out with a Fashion Merchandising degree. Not even halfway through my freshman year, my father asked about my major. When I told him, there was no encouragement or "good for you." I felt discouraged and foolish for my choice, so I changed it.

I was insecure and changed my major based not only on my father's opinion but on what others told me I should do. Although I had ideas and expressed them, I always seemed to back down whenever someone had a strong opinion. The people I hung out with influenced decisions, and my party lifestyle heavily affected my education. I picked a major, started the classes, could not make the grades, so I switched. My choices were General Studies, Communication, Psychology, Business, and finally back to Fashion Merchandising. I decided on Fashion because it seemed like the only classes I could pass.

I was not an outstanding student and needed the bare minimum requirements to graduate. It took five years, but I graduated and was so thankful. During my college internship at a women's boutique, I discovered I liked the merchandising part of the job but not dealing with the demanding, rich clients. I have learned over the years, through trial and error, what I do not want. I threw fashion out the window and did nothing with my major. Even with an education, I failed for years to use my knowledge and experience to take advantage of excellent opportunities that came along. It took a radical change to set me on a path to success.

BOYFRIENDS

I did not make good choices, especially with men. When I started dating at fourteen, it was always the "bad guys." What I learned over the years is bad meant they were broken, insecure, and acted out to get attention. They were no different from me, so I would have been considered a "bad girl." We were chasing the wrong things to find happiness and acceptance driven by instant gratification, perceived status, and materialism.

Sick people tend to attract other sick people. I wanted what they had and went after them. I dated the drug dealer, the college dropout, and a narcissist that used my brokenness to beef up his ego. There were few long-term relationships, probably because of my out-of-control drinking. Men probably noticed the big *danger* sign flashing above my head. Healthy people saw my miserable behavior and never called back. The bad guys latched on in the role of rescuer for the journey of dysfunctional codependency. I was submissive and easily drew someone who enjoyed being in a dominant role.

I had one long-term boyfriend in high school and was on and off with him in college. It was a toxic relationship. We cheated on each other and both had a tough time breaking it off. He was the drug dealer, and I could not see a long-term future with him, even though I fantasized about it for years. I often wondered, *Why do I stay with him?* He talked a lot about future goals and dreams but took little action. I also wanted something better, but for years did not change my behavior or shallow thinking.

The men I was interested in at college were ones I met bar tending or after the bar closed. I am here to tell you that nothing good happens after the bar closes, only more drinking and lots of drugs. I met guys at the bar because drinking and partying were all I did outside of work and school. I did not date many of them because partying, not dating, was my priority.

I worked at many bars, nightclubs, and restaurants throughout college. Because of the partying and how often I drank out of control and blacked out, I made bad choices and was promiscuous. I would meet someone at a bar, get drunk, and go home with them. Most times I woke up not knowing where I was, who I was with, or remembering what I had done. It only gave me an excuse to drink again to forget what happened. For five years in college, this was my dangerous lifestyle.

There are so many people who have experienced this tragic way of life. Maybe you know someone, or perhaps it is you. The addiction and lifestyle will only get worse if there is no decision to get help. My destructive journey continued, and I ultimately found the way out of it. But not before a series of events that became opportunities and led to a changed life.

PART THREE

DIGGING THE HOLE DEEPER

ALCOHOL MAGNETISM

My story is not a look back on life and how I could have done things differently. My vulnerability is about what did not work for me, how the domino effect of bad choices brought me to rock bottom, and the dramatic transformation that took place when I found a relationship with Jesus and put in the hard work to change. This section continues to show how addiction and poor choices impact not only our lives but those around us. I hope that if you relate to anything I say or have experienced, and you find yourself wanting to change your life or help someone you know, I am here to encourage and give you hope it is possible. The first step is recognizing there is a serious problem and admitting the need for help.

When I was in the middle of denial and an unmanageable life, it seemed completely normal to me. I thought I was amazing, life was good, and I did not need help of any kind. I was an egomaniac with an inferiority complex. I had low self-esteem and was extremely insecure, hiding behind a mask of superiority. Little did I know that selfish pride would cost me everything that had meaning and leave me emotionally bankrupt.

I married the first guy that liked the party girl persona I was selling at the strip club. Yes, I met my husband at a strip club. That is where I thought meaningful relationships start. I met Tony during summer break when I lived in Virginia, and he was a regular customer. I thought Tony was my knight in shining armor. Seemed like a great idea he liked to party and so did I. He was a policeman, and I thought he would take care of me, protect me from others, and keep my behavior in check. They say hindsight is 20/20, and looking back, my motives for marriage were as broken as I was. Tony appeared to have it all together, that is what he told me, and I believed it for all the years that we were together.

Tony and I had a blast together from the moment we met my last semester of college. We went out to the bars and partied every time he visited almost every week. I never got another driving under the influence charge because he drove me everywhere. By the time I met Tony at age twenty-one, I had been arrested four times within three years for drunken behavior in public and twice for DUI within six months of each other. I thought, *That happens in college. You party and sometimes get in trouble.* I never considered that I had a drinking problem, but now know it was the beginning of a downward spiral.

My denial about excessive drinking and habit of careless behavior carried over into every area of my life. My second DUI just before I met Tony was handled irresponsibly and shamefully. I did not have the money for the hefty lawyer bill and fine. I had no savings because after I paid the bills, every penny went to drinking. There was no money available on my credit cards. I called everyone I could think of to ask for the money, but no one helped me.

I felt there were no other options, the result of my sad and limited frame of mind. I chose to do something I said I would never do for money and stripped for two weeks doing double shifts, high on coke and drunk the entire time just to get through it. There was no way I could do that sober. There are consequences for our choices, and this experience was one of the lowest points of shame in my life. I cared more about what others thought of me than what I needed to do to help myself.

After I graduated from college, I moved to Northern Virginia and in with Tony. We dated four years before we got married. He was my party partner and the person who looked after me as my drinking escalated. He knew I drank alcoholically because we talked about it. We had an agreement to keep it under control––which only happened when I was at work events. After I left them and went home or to the local bar, I drank how I wanted to.

I worked hard to pay bills and partied hard as often as I could. Tony and I had fun until my functioning alcoholism changed and took over my life. Our relationship turned into dysfunctional codependency with caretaking, enabling, people pleasing, perfectionism, and guilt between us. We did not get the professional help we both needed, and the problems continued.

WHAT DO I WANT TO BE WHEN I GROW UP?

After college I still did not know what career I wanted to pursue. I continued to bartend part-time for about five years while I went from job to job. I started to sell health and life insurance door-to-door. That lasted nine months. The boss made a pass at me, and rather than stand up for myself and tell someone, I just quit. I allowed others to influence too much of my life.

The next job was an idea from a bar customer. We were talking about life and what I should do. They said, "I think you would be a great concierge." Within a couple of weeks, I got a job as a concierge at a fancy building in Washington, DC. That job lasted about six months when I realized I needed more money to afford my lifestyle. I talked to a college friend Amy who appeared to make a good living in Charlotte, North Carolina as a job recruiter. She made a few calls and after a couple of interviews, I started my career in IT staffing.

I loved this industry because I could make a lot of money if I did a good job. Even better, we got to drink a lot after work and entertain clients. This was awesome, and most of the time we did not have to pay for it. I could invite Tony and his food and drinks were paid for as well. It was a win-win for us!

I had arrived! Life for the next nine years was all about chasing the next party. I worked hard during the day so I could drink heavy at night. I went out with my work crew often and became fast friends with most of them. I was with the company for two years before a bully in the office made me feel uncomfortable. Once again, I did not stand up for myself and quit, leaving a decent job and a great boss. The pattern continued as I jumped around from job to job, leaving because someone made me uncomfortable, or I did not like the boss.

I was a functioning alcoholic for years. I always went to work and made my commitments, but it was a challenge to keep up with the demands and responsibilities while drinking heavily. It was an exhausting time in my life, but I chose it.

There were many volunteer and leadership roles I took on within the networking groups I was a part of that helped my sales job. I spent a few days a week either planning, leading, or attending networking functions or charity events. Thankfully I never tarnished my reputation attending or leading an event. I jammed my life with exercise, work, volunteering, and drinking.

Networking at a local bar one evening, I met my next boss, Robert. I seemed to be the right business development person for his company. When I started working, there were only a handful of us. I had little to no supervision in the office with rarely anyone ever there. I did what I needed to get done as quickly as possible so I could leave and go to the bar. This dangerous habit began my downward alcoholic spiral.

I eventually began to frequently leave early and sit at the bar for hours while I drank and worked. It was easy for me to leave as early as two or three o'clock because my boss Robert and I often drank together. Sometimes we had a lunch meeting with clients or just the two of us and start drinking. I spent a little over two years at the company and left because they downsized and no longer needed my role. Who knows, maybe they saw right through me and realized I was a liability. I will never know.

UNMANAGEABILITY AND DENIAL

I dabbled here and there with cocaine before meeting Tony and laid off it once we got together because I knew he did not approve. I was a dedicated pot head all through our relationship and into my thirties. I did hallucinogenic drugs just because they were around. I never got into pills, just never understood what so many liked about it. For that, I am grateful! I remember my mother telling me when I was a teenager, "Just lay off the hard drugs." That stuck with me, and I did.

Alcohol was my main addiction, and it was everything to me. I thought about it all the time and counted down the hours and minutes until I could take my first drink after work. I did not drink in the morning and just pushed through the hangover during the week. On weekends, I got together with friends for brunch, so it felt okay to drink if I was with others. There was a rare occasion when I drank alone because someone was always up for it. There were lots of drinking friends around at almost any time of day. Just before I got sober, I often drank alone, even sneaking beer which was not my drink of choice. It was all that was in the house, and I did not discriminate getting my buzz on.

Tony was not a bad person and there was never physical abuse, but over the years there was a lot of painful communication between us. I learned later through counseling and reflection how dysfunctional and codependent our relationship was. We had not learned good communication skills. I am sure I was a nightmare to deal with in my blackouts. Tony was not an alcoholic but did occasionally binge drink. I was sick and got worse while we were married and knew I was a functioning alcoholic for a few years before I got sober. I was okay with that level of alcoholism and so was Tony. Although he wanted me to get my drinking under control, he was not supportive when I did decide to quit.

Toward the end of my drinking addiction, I prayed when I left work, "Help me not to drive to the bar," but I could not overcome this destructive habit. I got mad at myself and asked, "How did I end up here? Why can't I just go home? I do not want to be here!" One day after losing the battle to not go to the bar, I found myself ordering a glass of wine and a shot of whiskey. The first sip of wine made me throw up, and I was so disgusted with myself. My body was physically rejecting the alcohol. I forced the shot down and the rest of the wine, closed my tab, and left. When I get an urge to drink now, this is one of the memories I replay in my mind. I go over in my head what will happen if I have just one drink. Thankfully it does not happen very often, but I have a list of examples like that to help keep me sober.

I did not drink every day because I occasionally used will power and self-control. It was my attempt to prove I was not an alcoholic, but it never lasted for more than a day or two. I always picked back up and the next black out happened. My will power eventually wore off, and I found myself at the gates of emotional hell.

Tony and I talked often about how my drinking was out of control. The conversations were like the movie "Groundhog Day" with the same words and actions repeated over and over. Everything I did revolved around where my next drink came from. The friends I picked, the jobs I accepted, and the vacations I went on all were driven by drinking. Most of the people I hung out with did not drink like me, but some did. That was always my saving grace because I pointed the finger toward them to take it off me. "See, I'm not as bad as Shelley. Did you see how she acted last night?" I brushed my behavior under the rug like it was no big deal.

I tried controlled drinking on and off for years, but it never worked. I told myself, *Do not drink much if I am in a bad mood. Do not drink much on an empty stomach. Do not drink dark liquor. Do not mix liquor and wine. Do not take more than four or five shots in one evening. Do not drink with more than one straw.* I liked to get a new straw for every drink, and sometimes

I had a drink with five, six, seven, or more straws! I thought, *Do not smoke pot and drink at the same time.* I knew getting high would take my buzz to the next level, and there came the black-out. I tried to control an addiction with rules that seemed reasonable but were not.

I was always chasing a feeling of numbing euphoria I had once as a teenager, until I finally gave up and got sober. I was a broken, scared little girl, and alcohol erased my hurtful feelings for years. Towards the end, I chased getting as wasted as I could as quickly as possible, and I did not care about anything else.

I put myself in situations many times that could have ended badly for me. One time I was at a party in Baltimore on a large boat with lots of people. I was drunk enough to slip and fall off the boat and into the water in the middle of the night. The water was freezing, and looking up I was under the boat. Next thing I knew someone jumped in and pulled me out before something terrible happened. These kinds of experiences were common when I drank, and I was always humiliating myself. I am sure Tony felt the same. How could he not? I was a walking embarrassment.

I kept a calendar every year from the time I was in high school. For the last three years of my drinking, I tracked the days I did drink. There were only a handful of days in the month that I did not drink and sometimes as few as three to five days. I guess seeing it on paper over and over did not sink in that my life was not normal, and I continued to drink anyway. I keep those calendars as a reminder of where I was and to never forget that all it takes is one drink to start the cycle that can lead to my death.

HEALTH GOING DOWN HILL

About a year before I quit drinking at age thirty-one, I was on a weekend trip to the beach to visit friends. I experienced my first panic attack and had no clue what it was or what was going on within my body. Everything inside tightened up, and I was gasping for air and felt like I was dying. The ambulance came and rushed me to the hospital. They hooked me up to an IV for a couple of hours until I was well enough to be released. The doctor questioned my alcohol consumption, and I lied and said, "I drink socially but do not have a problem."

I went back to the house where I was staying and drank again. It was a Super Bowl party, and I was not going to be left out of the fun. That is how sick I was. I thought, *There is nothing wrong with the way I drink.* Everyone close to me—but me—had an issue with my drinking.

My boss Robert is the person who gave me my first Xanax. It was the Tuesday morning following my weekend trip for the Super Bowl party. Robert and I went to lunch, and I told him my story and hospital visit. He gave me a couple of Xanax and said, "The next time you feel one coming on, take one of these. Panic attacks have sometimes happened to me after a night of drinking, and I take these when I feel one starting." I thought, *Oh, a magic pill to help me through a hangover. This is genius!* I went to my psychiatrist and said, "I need to get a Xanax prescription. My anti-anxiety meds are not helping, and I started experiencing panic attacks." I was surprised how easy it was to get the prescription.

I never told my psychiatrist about the drinking. My panic attacks continued, and she refilled the prescription. I took a Xanax every morning after a night of drinking because I could barely get out of bed to go to work. With a panic attack, I lost hours of the day because I needed a cool dark place to curl up and try to fall asleep. The attacks happened more often and continued for ten months until I quit drinking all together.

My primary care physician was a different story and had me figured out. For ten years I saw him for anxiety and high blood pressure. I was now thirty-one and had been taking anti-anxiety medication for seven years. It started because of a nervous stomach, but looking back it was when I worked hard and partied harder. That lifestyle was too much for me, and the medication helped to calm me down. The prescription was at the highest dosage level to work for me and only for my anxiety.

In my late twenties I also had hypertension and was prescribed blood pressure medication. Smoking a pack of cigarettes a day and being a heavy drinker escalated my health issues. The last few years before I got sober, my health was so bad that I was on three different medications to keep my blood pressure down.

With normal being less than 120 over 80, my blood pressure was 150-160 over 110-120. The last time I saw that doctor was a few months before I quit drinking. He said, "Kelly, I believe you have a drinking problem, and you need help." Over the years I lied to him, but I could no longer explain away the puffiness, bloated red face, and high blood pressure. He said bluntly, "You will have a stroke if you do not stop and need help before it is too late." He made a recommendation, and I let it go in one ear and out the other. I thought, *This man does not know what he is talking about* and never went back to him.

Along with the anxiety and high blood pressure I developed psoriasis and psoriatic arthritis. Maybe it was from genetics or being super active my entire life. It could have been the years of hard falls to my knees when I was drunk. Whatever the reason, it was painful. Psoriasis started to appear on my legs, arms, and face. It was awful, and I felt so insecure and self-conscious. The outbreaks continued to get worse the last year I drank. Once I quit, the psoriasis miraculously started to quickly go away. Imagine that.

Within three months of finally quitting alcohol, my physical injuries dramatically increased. I had been in the hospital three times with concussions from falling or banging my head. I often fell during blackouts. Sadly, I used to bang my head against the wall. I am not sure if it was to get attention, try to hurt myself, or look like a lunatic. I remember my mom hit her head the same way, so it makes sense that I repeated the behavior. Whatever the reason, I could have seriously hurt myself. I am grateful nothing permanent happened other than a small visible knot on my forehead that has thankfully reduced over time but is still very much present.

LIFESTYLE CHOICES

While married only a couple years, Tony and I made a choice one drunken evening that led to participating in an alternative lifestyle. Something that you only hear about in the movies, on talk shows, or in a group of people gossiping about someone you probably do not know. This led to years of dishonoring myself and my body.

One evening while partying at another couple's house, one action led to another and the next day I said out loud, "Did we really do that?" I waited for Tony's response and he said, "Yes, I liked it. Did you?" To me it did not matter what I thought. I only wanted to please him and said, "If that makes you happy, let's do it again."

The choice we made that day turned into a new lifestyle and a group of friends. I alienated myself from many of the friends I had for years. They did not agree with our new lifestyle and distanced themselves from us. I chalked it up to them being judgmental, and I was highly offended and my feelings badly hurt. I thought, *Why can they not realize this is good for my marriage?*

I told them and myself, "This makes our marriage so much better," not realizing the path I was on was terrible for someone like me that struggled with self-esteem, self-image, and self-respect.

I never shared with anyone what was really going on inside my head. I was not sure what I was thinking or if I was allowed to question our behavior. When I thought about what we were doing, the conflicting voices in my head were at battle. One voice told me, *You are being judgmental, and this is perfectly healthy for loving couples to do.* The other voice was, *You know this is not right.* Honestly, I could not think for myself. I did not have a mind of my own and wanted to please Tony. He was up for it if I was, so I went with it.

This lifestyle made for a lot of bad nights. I was very meek and "go with the flow" when I was not drinking. I did not confront people or speak my mind until I was drunk and more often when I was blackout drunk. Then I was downright belligerent and mean. Lots of shame and guilt always came after the wild nights. In my heart I knew it was wrong for me. In my stomach I felt the anxiety that always came with it. But I brushed it under the rug and drank my way through the nights and most of the next mornings. I acted like it was no big deal and completely normal to hook up with other couples. I coped by drinking my feelings away and kept moving forward by acting like everything was awesome and life was fun.

I hooked up with Tony, men, and women, so I came to the conclusion that I was bisexual and thought, *If I am doing this, then that is what it means.* My mind could not process what I was doing because I was always under the influence during the acts. I had girlfriends on the side and brought them home. Then something would change inside me, and I immediately became angry and upset with what was happening and ruined the night. This went on for a while until I wrecked friendships from my outbursts.

The resentment, jealousy, and guilt were eating away inside me. It caused a lot of fights and turmoil in my relationship with Tony and others. The drinking during those years was ridiculous. I was always the drunkest at the parties. In some way I knew if I were out of it, people would not mess with me. The next day I got yelled at for my behavior, but I did not care.

There was a lot of justification of why we chose this lifestyle. It brought us closer and made Tony love me more. It made our relationship stronger. When others want you, it makes you more attractive to your partner. There was a lot of glitz, fun, and excitement about that life, and I became friends with some great people. Yet, I felt shame, remorse, and pretended to hide behind someone I was not. There was a good amount of jealousy, resentment, lying, and cheating also going on. I thought, *Other couples make it look so easy.* It did not work in our favor at all.

EMOTIONAL BANKRUPTCY

Nobody I ever met or have known gave up drinking on a winning streak. I am proud of who I am today and would scream it from the rooftops if nobody gave me crazy looks. I did not know and never once thought that life could be so wonderful compared to how I had lived for years. Just before I quit drinking, I was in bad shape physically and mentally. I had hit an all-time low and was emotionally bankrupt. I was a raging alcoholic, my marriage was totally dysfunctional, and I hated to come home every day. My only interests were to numb how I feel and be with my dogs.

I could not come home to Tony without feeling like I was walking on eggshells. I understand why he had no respect for me and do not blame him. I caught him texting other women, and I was done with life. I fought with Tony just to get attention.

I felt overwhelmed by my alcoholism. The doctor's words about a stroke and deteriorating health got to me. The shame was an awful burden to carry, and the conversations over and over with Tony about uncontrolled drinking were depressing and frustrating. I came to a crossroads and decided there were only two options--end my life or change.

My life had been destructive for over twenty years, and I was scared and did not know what to do or how to change. Suicide was not the answer, but it did not stop the devil from putting those thoughts in my head and considering them. Self-pity and fear of failure drove these harmful thoughts. I did not believe I could physically stop drinking or change, even if I wanted to. My addiction to alcohol caused terrible shakes without it, but I decided to try one more time to quit. I was terrified what would happen if I failed again and did not know it would be the worst experience of any other attempt to stop.

MY TRAGIC LOSS

The most tragic event in my life to date happened when I was at the beginning of my attempt to stop drinking. There had been three years of going back and forth with the thoughts in my head about controlled drinking or learning how to drink reasonably. I chose the first day of December as the day I would quit.

There is a back story that led to this event. You might agree that I was not responsible enough to bring children into this world. I thought a child would help me slow down, but Tony did not allow one into my alcoholic lifestyle. He did, however, allow me to rescue dogs.

It started with Raider. He was a beautiful white with black brindle coat American bulldog, also known as a pit bull. I got him as a puppy, and he was the sweetest dog and grew to be close to eighty pounds. Raider went to dog training, and I took him to play dates to socialize with other dogs. He was my first fur child, and I hit the jackpot. He was submissive to every dog and human he met. He was a great example of what a pit bull can be if raised correctly. Raider meant the world to me.

About a year later, Tony brought a dog home he found at work. He was another pit bill but much smaller than Raider. We named him Duke, and after slowly introducing them with the advice of outside help, the two got along well. They played together, slept together, and ate side by side. I was so happy that I was doing something right by these two rescues. I wanted to give them a good life, and they had it with us.

Another pit bull named Lady was brought to us to foster a couple of years later. We eventually adopted her, and the dynamics completely changed. The dogs became reactive and aggressive towards each other and it escalated over the next two years. We did everything we could––spent thousands of dollars on training, separated them from eating together, kept them caged up, and switched them in and out. Anything we read we tried, except re-homing them. Tony and I argued to re-home Lady, and it did not happen. After several dog fights, thousands of dollars in vet bills, and even a trip to the ER for me when I was breaking them up, the worst day happened.

I had been a few days sober since the beginning of December 2014, and I came home to let the dogs out. I do not remember, and it does not make sense how all three got out, but I must not have secured one of the cages correctly. Duke and Lady attacked Raider, and I tried everything to break them up. I opened the back door to separate them, and the dogs overpowered me.

Duke and Lady chased Raider outside my house and down the flight of stairs. I called Tony at once because I needed help. I screamed and cried at the top of my lungs, all the while hitting the dogs and pulling on them to stop. The few minutes this went on seemed like hours. I am sure the neighbors could hear my screams for help.

Tony rapidly showed up and swooped in like the Incredible Hulk to separate them. We quickly wrapped Raider in towels and put him in the car. I repeatedly played in my head, *How did I let this happen? What did I do wrong? We had a plan, and it had been working.* I do not recall if the other two dogs went to the emergency vet except Raider where he had already been seen for many fights.

I also had to go to the hospital. While trying to break up the fight, three fingers were pretty chewed up and mangled. A bleeding hole in my right-hand needed to be stitched back together. I was in shock and felt nothing.

I told Tony, "The cost is not a worry. Do whatever it takes to bring Raider home." We agreed because we loved Raider. He was our first baby, and we needed him to come out of this okay. Four days went by, and they were all a blur. We made a heartbreaking mutual decision after the vet told us, "I'm so sorry about Raider. It's time to let him go and put him down. He will never be the same happy and playful dog again."

Being so early in sobriety and only seven days without alcohol, I had gained no coping skills. I relapsed and drank hard for days. The days were such a blur, and I am certain there were drugs involved. I remember very little of what happened or who I was with. There were lot of suicidal thoughts, and I remember standing outside on my second-floor deck staring down at the ground, wanting to jump off with Satan telling me, "Do it!"

There were horrible thoughts about myself. *I'm a loser. I'm such a failure. It was my fault, and I killed my beloved dog.* I blamed myself and thought suicide would be the right decision.

I remember Tony's words rang in my head, "You are a loser alcoholic like your father. You will never change." I just sat there and took it all in, swallowing his condemnation as the truth that this was my life forever. Thankfully, that was not God's truth about me or His plan for my future.

PART FOUR

LEARNING TO LIVE IN GOD'S WILL

LEARNING TO LIVE IN GOD'S WILL

I used to believe that people make you happy. Advertising, society, and the movies show us that. The belief that we find love and *live happily ever after* is not my experience and many people I know. When I got divorced and was alone--truly alone for the first time and sober--it was a new beginning with no outside influence of people telling me what to think or do. I had always believed in God, and a new journey began where I allowed Him to work in my life to change me.

Over the next two years, a seemingly impossible transformation took place. I began to say, "I truly love my life, being alone, and content with who I am becoming." There was a new understanding I did not need others to fill the hole of loneliness and rejection I had carried in my heart for years.

I told God and myself, "If I find a man to commit to, he will need to be amazing. He will have his own life and be a whole person. He cannot be broken and need rescuing or fixing." I knew this person had to add to my enjoyable and rich life and not diminish it or bring me down. I needed someone to lift me up and encourage me to walk in the purpose God gave me. This new beginning was a blessing, especially during my recovery from alcohol.

WALKING INTO RECOVERY

About a week after Raider passed, I started going for a few months to an outpatient rehab three times a week. In between rehab, I attended recovery meetings and asked Tony to come with me, but he refused. I cried and was scared because I was all alone. With badly shaking hands from withdrawals, I could barely fill out the paperwork. I was in so much pain and despair, and I wanted something different and was willing to do anything to change.

The withdrawals and shaking lasted about six weeks. It was dangerous to stop drinking without medical supervision, but I did not know any better. Looking back, I know God carried me through that time and kept me safe. In my mind, I thought I was alone in this hard process, but God was always with me.

We had family visits once a week at the rehab, and I felt hurt Tony never came. I left him and moved out of the house after only three weeks sober. I do not believe I would have left Tony or the house if Raider had been alive because the dogs kept me there. Raider dying made me realize it was the final straw for our destructive marriage and time to cut ties. It was a tough decision, but something had to change, and that would be me.

I was heartbroken, and my life was in shambles. The marriage was not worth fighting for, and to start over was easier than to stay. I felt empty inside and thank God for a few girlfriends. Jenessa allowed me to move in with her and was truly a godsend.

She was loving and encouraging every day I was at her home. Her confidence and strength rubbed off on me, even when I was pretending, and worked when it needed to.

For years, I had lived in a dark place and was surrounded by the wrong people. My confidence came from them. I mimicked what they did and took on their thoughts, feelings, and actions without knowing any different. I never had a mind of my own, and now know I could not escape the dark places without letting those people go and focus on God. The confidence, understanding of who I am, and answers about how to live that I searched for did not come from relying on others. It comes from God alone and is found in His Word, the Bible.

Fast forward two years to age thirty-four, and I am two years sober and in a twelve-step recovery program. My sponsor, Jen, helped me learn vital growth areas in my life that my parents should have taught me. They never learned important life skills like communication and decision making, so how would they know to pass them on to me? And if they knew, they never shared it.

I learned how to live life as it came to me and stay in my lane and mind my own business. Recovery taught me how to love and tolerate others for who they are without trying to change them. I learned how to pause and pray before speaking. I can now share my experiences with others and help them.

When I learn something new, I like to say, "I am growing through it." There were pivotal moments in the first few years of recovery where I suddenly thought, *Here is something new! Write it down, read it out loud, process it, and start practicing it.* I felt like I was on a hotel elevator, and at each level I went through every room on that floor to learn all I could, and then be ready to go to the next level. Recovery for me has been a floor at a time––sometimes stuck on one for a while––but always determined to get to the next level.

I constantly learn new ways to think and act. For example, for most of my life I thought my mother was selfish and abandoned me in the years I needed her the most. Today I understand that my mother did the best she knew how with what she had been taught and capable of. Now that I know better, I also can do better. I give grace to others because it is the right way to think and act.

The real recovery journey is the one that takes place within us, not the physical act of quitting. Stopping the alcohol was only the beginning because I had to dig deep in my soul and be willing to share everything to recover and renew my mind. I shared what happened, how it made me feel, and how it has affected me over the years. I took trauma from my childhood and brought it into all the relationships I had because I did not know better.

Alcohol was a symptom of the problem. My thinking was the issue, and I had to unlearn a lot. Some principles I had to learn from scratch because of the ideas and words I had never heard of. Many of them I still practice today.

A few new issues have cropped up writing this book that I am digging into and working on. This is my journey of recovering life with God. I will never reach perfection, but I will become better each day because I am willing.

SURRENDER

When people think of surrender, many ideas come to mind. In a movie when police shout, "Put your hands up," the criminal does that to *physically surrender* or give up to authority. There is also *spiritual surrender* that is letting go of our own ways to a higher power. For me, to spiritually surrender is to align my thoughts, words, and actions with God's intentions in my daily life. It took a lot of practice to get to where I am today, and I still pursue this daily to live in God's will. In the Lord's prayer "<u>Thy will</u> be done on earth as it is in Heaven "means God's will, not Kelly's. This is no longer the "Kelly Show" because God is now in control.

I have not always been a Christ follower. I always believed there was a God to pray to, but I was one of those people that did "fox hole prayers" to get me out of a DUI or promised I would not drink ever again if He took the hangover pain away. I never had an intimate relationship with Jesus Christ until I invited Him into my heart and soul. That came after I quit drinking, and someone shared with me I could have a personal relationship with the God of my understanding.

When you have that relationship, it doesn't mean your problems go away. The truth is, you have a God who is always there to help you through them. If you want that relationship too, all you need to do is pray this prayer.

Heavenly Father, I believe that Jesus Christ, the Son of God, came to earth to be the Savior of the world. By His death on the cross, He paid the price for the sin of the world, and that whoever believes in Him will not perish, but have everlasting life.

My God is loving, forgiving, tolerant, protective, a teacher, a listener, and a healer. He healed my sickness of alcoholism that I have had since I was nineteen. God removed the obsession to drink, and that is a miracle. I gave my whole heart and soul over to Him to do with as He wishes and want to serve God every day for the rest of my life because of what He did for me. I want to make my heavenly Father proud of me, and my goal each day is to grow toward God's will. He knows that my will has never worked over the many years I tried to control my way through life.

I learned early in my walk with the Lord that surrendering is not a onetime occurrence. It is a daily decision and can sometimes occur many times throughout the day as I release my control over the person or situation. It is a conscious choice to surrender and allow for God's will.

There are days I realize I am trying to take control and throw my hands in the air and speak out loud, "Okay, God. I am giving this person or situation to You. I release it to You and Your will." If I want to keep my peace of mind, I know that is what I am supposed to do. When I am in the middle of a busy day and trying to accomplish more than one person can alone, I must pause and ask myself, *Am I living in God's will or my will?* God has a plan for my life and does not want me to over commit myself day after day.

My first memory of spiritual surrender was from 2014. It was a couple of weeks before the incident with Raider. I was on my hands and knees, crying in my closet. This was the place I went to hide from Tony, but I am sure he had some idea of what I was doing. I went there to hide my drinking, drugging, crying, and to bang my head against the wall––a sick form of punishment when I hated my situation or myself. I remember crying out to God, "Help me! I do not know how to change. I give up Lord, I give up! Please help me and fix me. I cannot do this anymore."

Something happened at that moment I cannot explain. I felt a peace and calm came over me I was going to be okay. It was my burning bush experience. If you are not familiar with the term *burning bush,* my interpretation is it is a sign of God's presence in your life. I was in a bush with flames all around me, and God did not allow me get hurt. Instead, He gave me grace and a glimpse of the miracle He was about to perform in my life. Both a miracle and God's grace gave me that calming peace. I could vaguely see myself in the fire and Him protecting me.

That moment and feeling gave me hope, and I hung onto it! I let go and released my will––my entire will––and allowed God to take control. If spiritual surrender is what you desire for your life, you must be willing to change and do things differently so that God can move in your life. You cannot limit God to conditions that work for you, but truly release control to Him. I promise it will be the best decision you ever make!

The Bible says in Matthew 16:25, "For whoever wants to save their life will lose it, but whoever loses their life for Me will find it." This verse speaks so much to my soul because I felt like I lost my whole life when I surrendered to God. I left behind everything that was familiar and that felt safe. My home, marriage, pets, friends, and daily routine.

I went through a grieving process. A loss is painful, and it takes time for God to heal us. You may not forget all the pain, but you do not feel it inside as much anymore. Each person is unique, and some pain fades more quickly than other pain. Thankfully, God is always there to help you through it.

The second part of the verse "but whoever loses their life for me will find it," happened to me! I lost my old life of poor decisions and shame, and God helped me to create a new life of peace, purpose, and confidence. The Lord has blessed me more than I could ever dream of. The peace I have today in my heart is indescribable, and it started when I surrendered to God and began to work on myself.

Have you ever felt impending doom? When you add addiction, chaos, and drama together, you get impending doom. Before my decision to surrender and change, there was always the looming feeling of waiting for something bad to happen or that everything was about to fall apart. Every morning I woke up and wondered what I did, who I upset, or the dreaded phone call from someone telling me what I did the night before.

I have not had that awful feeling in years, but if I think about those memories too long, the heaviness and panic can start to quickly take over. When that happens, I need to stop and surrendered my life over to God again and that His will to be done. Impending doom has no place in my life. I never want to go back to that person I was or the horrible place I was in.

GIVE IT TO GOD

"Come to me, all you who are weary and burdened, and I will give you rest. Take my yoke upon you and learn from me, for I am gentle and humble in heart, and you will find rest for your souls" (Matthew 11:28-29 NIV).

Taking ownership of everything I had done over the years was hard, but it was necessary for me to do and part of my growth process. I got to the point where I hated the person I was and mad at myself for all that I had done. Relationships were damaged, no self-respect, and I was in total despair. I carried a heavy shame and burden. It was critical as part of my recovery work to get honest with myself. I learned I do not have to carry the sin and burden any longer. The reason is...I just need to give it to Jesus, and He will carry it!

Say what? God will do that for me? But how do you give it to God? I recall early in sobriety someone saying, "Jesus is all you need. He died for your sins and is waiting for you to give Him your life." I could not comprehend the words I heard. I had a blank stare, and all I could think was, *Okay, please explain yourself, Lord. I am listening.* As I searched for understanding, I saw it in my mind. I am holding my problem, situation, issue, control, or whatever it is in my hands. I always want to control what is going on, including the beginning, middle, and outcome. When I let go, I release my control, my will, and the outcome over to God to do His part and will. My responsibility is to do what I can, which is to take care of my thoughts and actions. I cannot control any person or situation except for me and stay on my side of the street.

I make the effort, and God produces the results. When I do the right thing, I can rest knowing that whatever the outcome, it will happen God's way. I can learn from it and grow, even if it is not the outcome I wanted. God has a plan, and it is far greater than my own. I know this because He has proven it repeatedly since that day in 2014 when I surrendered to Him. All I do is hand it over, and He will do the rest.

HAVING A VOICE/MIND OF MY OWN

Have you ever heard, "If I want your opinion, I will <u>ask</u> for it"? I never had an opinion of my own because what I heard in my mind from people was, *If I <u>want</u> your opinion, I will <u>give</u> it to you.* Someone always had something to say about my ideas and opinions, and I still sometimes struggle with it.

My first memory of saying something on my mind was about four or five and at the babysitter's. I know I was that young because this sitter was in Virginia, and we did not move to West Virginia until after I was five. I was playing with the other children, and it was getting close to pick up time. There was a TV show called *Fat Albert* that we watched. A father showed up for his child, and he reminded me of the cartoon character. Me being a kid, I just repeated what I heard from the jolly catchy phrase and said, "Hey, hey, hey, it's Fat Albert." Almost immediately my arm was yanked, I was pulled into the bathroom, and a bar of soap was shoved into my mouth. I remember crying and wondering what I had done. The babysitter said harshly, "Do not to speak and keep your mouth shut!" From then on, I was always cautious of what I said because I was afraid of how it would be received or rejected.

If you think your own voice does not matter, it is far from the truth. I was stuck in a negative mindset for so long and never knew that it was wrong. The truth was, I could have my voice, choice, and opinions. All the times I was molested, I believed I did not have a voice and just sat or laid there frozen. I never owned my thoughts because I believed they were stupid or crazy. Over time, I have learned to look at life from a different perspective.

As a child, I picked sports based on what other people wanted for me. I wanted to take ballet and dance, and I ended up with baseball and karate like my brother. Maybe my mom wanted me to do what my brother did, or she did not have the time to drive us around to different activities and chose what we could do together. Either way, Mom decided for me.

When I was in college, a Presidential election was going on, and I was excited to vote for the first time. God forbid I share my opinion with others because as soon as I opened my mouth, I was usually chastised and made to feel like an idiot. I voted based on my friends' beliefs because mine were stupid. If I were in a group of friends, and someone I liked was being gossiped about, I never stood up for them for fear of being criticized.

When Tony and I married, we had the option to have a religious ceremony. Tony did not want one, and although I felt it was wrong, I went with what he wanted. Throughout our marriage, I always took on his beliefs. If I had an opinion, he usually spoke over me with his ideas and I thought, *Well, that sounds better than mine, so I will just believe what he does.* He was not into church and told me, "Keep your beliefs to yourself" anytime I wanted to talk to him about God, and I went to church by myself. He did not like certain friends of mine, and when I adopted the thoughts and opinions he had of them, I lost a few friends I enjoyed spending time with.

About a year and a half after I was sober, I met a guy in my apartment complex, and he invited me over for coffee. I told him, "I want to get to know you, be friends, and that is it." Within ten minutes of sitting down, he was all over me with kissing and groping me. I said, "I do not want to do this and only want to be friends." He ignored me and kept on until it was over. I felt so defeated inside. I set a boundary, vocalized it, and he completely shut me down. He ignored my boundaries and had his way. I just laid there and prayed for God to protect me. My thought was always, *If I fight back, it will be worse than if I just lay here.* I was so mad at myself and said, "How did this happen again? Why do people not listen to me? What did I do wrong?" The lesson I learned was if I never went to his apartment, that could not have happened.

When I met my husband Dave, I was able to express my voice. He is so wonderful because Dave genuinely wants me to grow. He will always ask my opinion and ask me to think it through. Sometimes when he asks me, I think, *Why are you asking me this?* He knows what is important to me and says, "I value your opinion." Now, that is a good man. I love how the growth areas that are valuable to me are important to him.

I had conflicted beliefs most of my adult life about having children. At one point I wanted them so I could take my focus off drinking. Then I wanted them to save my marriage. I said to some people, "I left Tony because he did not want a family." When I dated in sobriety, I told people, "I want a family."

I never really knew if I wanted children or if it was because society told me I should to be happy. I even pushed Dave away a month after dating because he could not have any more kids. One of my self-help books said, "If you do not have children of your own, God can replace them with other fruit." That happened in my life. When I married Dave, I became a *bonus* mom and have two great adult children. The fruit in my life is the women I can touch with my experience.

MANIPULATION AND CONTROL

Manipulation sounds so derogatory and negative, and that is how I lived for an awfully long time. My perspective was, "How can I use you to gain something in return?" I wanted to make myself appear in a more positive light and did not think of it as manipulation. I can now see how the schemes and tactics scream I was an expert at it.

I had to learn to surrender manipulation and control like so many other behaviors I had to let go of. Surrender is a *choice*, and you can surrender yourself, your will, and other people. Turning people over to God can be difficult because you want the best for them.

In my former life, I wanted to control outcomes. Controlling others through manipulation was something I was particularly good at, and in recovery I had to unlearn it. A phrase that a good friend shared with me is, "What others do is not my concern and none of my business." I constantly remind myself of that simple statement. I am learning to "stay in my lane," or one I like is "stay in my hula hoop."

I cannot control the choices and outcomes of other people's lives. Although I sure tried for a long time, I am not to play God. There was a constant fight for something I wanted, and it was wrong. I know others must make their own choices––whether good or bad––and stay out of it. I have learned that I must surrender others to God for His will to be done. It is their life and my part is to pray for them and God's will.

Surrender is not something that happens overnight, and it takes practice. When I find myself trying to control a situation or an outcome, I check myself and go to God and ask for forgiveness. He knows better than I do, and His plan is always best in the end. Want to make God laugh? Tell Him the plans you have for your life.

I learned how to control others from watching my mother. She controlled me through manipulation. She also controlled by withholding love if I did not do something she liked. Mom bought me things in return for doing something she wanted me to. I often missed school so she had someone to go shopping with. School was not a priority like shopping, and that pattern followed me through college and my twenties.

Debt was a bad habit I picked up from my mom that I had to unlearn in recovery. I was good at maxing out credit cards. I went through debt consolidation, got out of debt after a few years, maxed them out again, and consolidated my debt again. My dangerous habit did not end the first time, and I had to repeat the process again.

It took years of practice and learning what worked for others, and I now have excellent credit. Do you see the pattern? Everything I did was wrong, and I had to learn how other people were successful in different areas of their life. I now have a healthy fear of not buying anything I cannot afford and pay off that same month. This new habit brings me a lot of peace and contentment.

BLAME AND SHAME

"Everything you do is based on the choices you make. It is not your parents, your past relationships, your job, the economy, the weather, an argument, or your age that is to blame. You and only you are responsible for every decision and choice you make. Period."

--Wayne Dyer

I do not think it is any coincidence that blame and shame rhyme. They directly result from choices and decisions that are made by you and me. Blame was a close companion of mine for years. It made me the victim, and I felt comfort from branding myself in that role.

Being a victim was a safe space for me to hide and not be responsible for anything. I liked the attention when I shared my victimization with others. When I lived in that mentality, I did not know any better or realize how unhealthy and troubling that thinking was. I did not want to hear, "Remaining a victim is unhealthy for you" and thought, *How dare you discredit what happened to me?* I would say, "I am a victim" and do nothing to change. Being a victim was a great excuse to drink when all the others had run out.

In college I blamed drinking on "That's what college kids do." We went out to clubs, frat parties, and tailgated before games. I was like every young college adult, right? After I left college and had a regular job, I blamed my crazy drinking nights on a difficult day at work, a bully, a friend being mean to me, and anything I could think of––except me. How could I be the problem?

I criticized my parents for my actions or choices because I was never taught any better. I carried around blame for them for varied reasons, and that victim attitude followed me through my teenage years to early thirties.

I created excuses for my alcoholism by saying, "My dad is an alcoholic." Not because I saw him drunk, but that is what my mom called him. I just figured, "I picked up the alcoholic gene." I saw my dad on weekends until I was about five years old and holidays through my teenage years. We did not have a close, functioning relationship, and that made it easier to believe my alcoholism was his fault.

It was my sobriety that eventually led to a breakthrough between Dad and me. I worked on myself and the issue of acceptance, and I began to accept Dad for who he was and what he was capable of. After many counseling sessions and the work I did with Jen, our relationship started to flourish. Hallelujah, praise the Lord, I now have what I had longed for so many years––a healthy relationship with my dad! We talk on the phone often, and he comes to visit me. We have the rest of our lives to create good memories.

As I wrote this chapter, I prayed for God to reveal to me anything from my past I could share that was relevant to blame. I figured God knows my story better than I do, and why not go straight to the source? He showed up for me not even a day later. An old friend, Jamie, I had not seen in over eight years sent me a text message. It read, "Kelly, your posts are truly inspiring. Keep it up. Please let me know if you are in the area! I would love to catch up. Love you."

This message was like a light bulb went off. I blamed her for years for something she did not even do. We lived with her parents the summer before my last semester of college. We worked together at a bar in DC and carpooled together on the days we shared shifts. It was common for us cocktail servers to drink with customers while working our shifts. Our agreement was whoever was driving did not drink or drink very little.

One night after a shift and my turn to drive, I got pulled over for speeding. After a sobriety test, the officer told Jamie, "If you drive home, then she will not go to jail. Poor Jamie said, "I do not know how to drive a stick shift and cannot get us home." That night I was arrested and went to jail.

I firmly told myself, *My DUI is all Jamie's fault! If she had just magically figured out how to drive a stick shift, she would have gotten us back home to continue our lives.* How delusional for me to think that way! I took my actions and consequences and assigned the fault to her. It made me sad to realize what a selfish friend I was. I am thankful that I now have the awareness to take responsibility for my thoughts, words, and actions.

My delusional thinking often got ridiculous and shows that God can change anyone, no matter how messed up their life is. I was traveling to Charlotte, NC for the 2010 4th of July to visit one of my girlfriends. I went to the airport early thinking I could get an earlier flight. I never thought about it being a holiday weekend, and to my surprise the airport was packed. I went to the bar and started drinking right away. My flight got delayed, and I continued to drink for about six to eight hours. I staggered onto the plane and to my seat. The flight attendant came up and quietly said, "I'm sorry, but you will have to get off the plane." I was too drunk and a liability. I immediately went to the main desk to complain, rejected drinking as the reason, and blamed the flight attendant for kicking me off. My delusional thinking was obvious, and I got nowhere and left once again as a victim.

I was stuck in the shame and blame cycle for many years. I shared with friends and complete strangers my private issues to get people to feel sorry for me and usually did this in a drinking atmosphere, where they coddled me and often bought me drinks. I had years of experience doing this because drinking was my life from eighteen to thirty-two years old. Those poor bartenders probably thought, *Oh look out, here comes the hot mess walking in the door* instead of *Here comes Kelly again. Wow, she has her life totally together.*

I sometimes wonder if the people I hung out with even liked me, or because they felt sorry for me. Either way, it is in the past and I am not that person anymore. I have learned that I could not get better if I continued behavior that held me back. Blame became a way of life and was no longer old behavior, but a habit I had to let go of.

I first blamed others in counseling. I was twenty-one, and the court ordered counseling right after my first DUI. It was my first time in it, and I got to share my feelings with someone who did not know me. I focused on how others hurt me rather than on drinking as my way to cope through life. The DUI directly resulted from my actions, I did not accept ownership of those actions, and I had to deflect the attention off me and put it on others.

It started with pointing the finger at my dad. I liked the feeling of pity and do not know if I felt it from the counselor. There was comfort in the self-pity I created. I thought, *Poor me. My dad was not part of my life like I thought he should be, and he abandoned me. Poor me. My mother was not the present doting mother I expected and needed her to be.*

Abandonment and neglect from my parents were real and traumatic for me, but talking without action prevents healing and progress. Years of counseling went by, but I still coped with alcohol and excuses. I never processed my feelings or learned how to handle life without trying to control everything and everyone. I had to ask God to help me with forgiveness, understanding, and wisdom.

Self-pity and blame can create some twisted thoughts and lies, and there were a lot of them I believed about myself. I was not worthy of love but just a pretty face to be seen and not heard. I was for people to use and abuse and would never find true happiness. Satan was hard at work.

I laugh at myself sometimes when the old thoughts pop in my head. Even though God has made me a new person, the old patterns still occasionally creep in. The difference now is my awareness. A thought can come in, but I process it as a lie and toss it out. The troubling thoughts no longer have a place to stay in my head. I often laugh out loud and think, *Lord, thank you for delivering me from that lie.*

There are reasons why I became the person I was, but it did not give me the right to blame people. We all have free will, and I lived many years making poor choices every step of the way and did not want to be accountable for any of it. No one forced my decisions, and I still cast blame to take the focus off me and how I was truly living in the wrong with my confused and sinful thinking.

Before I married Tony, we discussed my alcohol issue. I do not know what he was thinking, but he still married me. A person with healthy boundaries would have stopped dating me. I was good at deflecting and downplaying the severity of my drinking. We were textbook codependent with Tony playing the role of both caretaker and hero and me being the needy alcoholic. Tony rarely shared what really went on behind closed doors and said, "No one needs to know our business." We seemed like a perfect *Ken and Barbie* couple, and that is what some friends called us.

People repeatedly scolded me the day after a night of binge drinking. I cried and made excuses for how I ended up so drunk––falling or embarrassing myself or someone I was with. During my drinking years, the frequent question I asked was, "What did I say or what happened?" because most of the time I blacked out. I then went straight to blaming my past sexual abuse, daddy issues, or whatever came to mind justifying the night before. Lying and manipulation took the focus off me so I could protect my love––alcohol addiction. I never admitted the common denominator in all the situations was my drinking and that I had a problem. After years of this, I am sure the excuses and same stories got old. Just writing this makes me annoyed with how I acted. What a disturbing way to live!

By now you can probably imagine some of the common excuses I repeatedly used.

"If you had my life, you would drink the same way. I was molested by multiple people before I was even a teenager. It makes sense I turned out to be a promiscuous adult."

I used sex in early sobriety as a replacement from the alcohol. I chalked it up to, "Well at least I am not drinking."

It cannot be that bad. "I did the best I could with what I knew how to do. If you went through the abandonment and rejection I felt, you would understand why I do what I do. That person really sent me over the edge last night, and I drank to cope with how they made me feel."

They made me feel was a common response I used to deflect. In general, deflection means you pass something over to someone to draw attention away from yourself. It is a psychological defense to deflect blame to others.

It took time, self-development, and practice to stop saying that phrase. I *choose* to feel a certain way. No one can make you feel anything if you do not allow it. Before I go to crazy town in my head, that often leads to blame and other outrageous scenarios I create, I can go to God and pray about a feeling. I find when the phrase "you made me feel" comes out of my mouth, I stop and say out loud, "Kelly, no one can make you feel that way." I must redirect myself and where my head is. An unhealthy habit developed over the years can take just as long to break. Practice, practice, and more practice is needed! Awareness of your thoughts is key, and it prevents actions that require an apology.

There were experiences that happened as a child that I was not responsible for. Over time, they affected my behavior, and I blamed others instead of getting the help I needed. The memories of being molested have played over and over in my head throughout my life. "How did this happen to me? How could someone take advantage of a child like that?" Nobody protected me from it, and as I got older was furious about it.

I did not learn physical boundaries, and as an adult became promiscuous. As a people pleaser, I went along with whatever others wanted so I could gain approval. I wanted to be liked by people I had just met. I allowed men to push themselves on me, even after I set up a boundary with them. In my mind I knew what I did not want, but the word "No" never made it out of my mouth. I thought in a dysfunctional way, but that was all I knew.

I learned through counseling and recovery that it is common behavior for victims of sexual abuse to become promiscuous and put themselves in reckless and dangerous environments. It is typical that when you go through life with little to no voice, to gain one is difficult, but possible with help and practice.

With an unhealthy mind, I blamed my childhood abusers for my reckless adult behavior. Who I became was the natural progression of an abused child that grew up and did not learn better. I did the best I could with what I knew, and it was not normal or healthy, and quite dangerous. I made the choice to put myself in situations and then felt fear, regret, and shame afterwards. Drinking was a way to forget what happened. Sometimes I blocked it out like nothing happened, which was easier than beating myself with, "You acted that way again!"

There is a reality called "drinking at people." It is a type of revenge or retaliation towards someone if they do something you do not like. I was a champion at drinking at people! Someone would upset me, and I retaliated by drinking. It was my defense mechanism to throw punches. Drinking did not just hurt me, but it hurt the people I was with because they had to experience my foolish behavior and sometimes be put in harmful situations. All I thought about was me, and everything I did was selfish.

Today I strive to live a blameless life, not blaming others for my behavior. The Bible says, "Blessed are those whose ways are blameless, who walk according to the law of the Lord" (Psalm

119:1). I want to please my heavenly Father. My prayer to Him in living a blameless life is "Please Lord God, I pray for truth in my heart to overpower casting blame. When it crops up, I will humble myself to make it right and live the life you have for me."

Just because I strive to live a blameless life does not mean it always happens. I am not by any means perfect, and when I catch myself acting in old behavior, I quickly fess up. Awareness is paramount in my healing journey.

Out of my shame, I blamed people for my actions to make it seem like they caused my drinking. I excessively drank because I had a problem with alcohol. Once I took a drink, I could not control how much I had or when to stop. I drank that way pretty much from the beginning of my destructive habit, am certain I was destined to be an alcoholic, and today I am okay with that. It is a chapter in my story, but it is certainly not the end.

I do not believe being an alcoholic is any different from me being severely allergic to a food or medicine. I had a bad reaction when I drank, and awful things happened. I have accepted my alcoholism and moved on to what I <u>can</u> control-- to wake up and <u>not</u> drink today. What I can control is how I react to life.

If you struggle like me with alcohol, sexual abuse, eating disorders, a failed marriage, abandonment, or rejection, there is a solution! First off, I am terribly sorry about what has happened to you. Second, you are not alone. Go to rehab, a counselor, to church, a twelve-step meeting, any recovery program--just do something different from what you are currently doing. I would not recommend doing it alone. You are not that powerful, and there is strength in numbers. I am a perfect example of trying to do it alone and failing miserably.

In the end, God is what worked for me. He directed me to the recovery formula that still works today. God is always willing to help, and combined with my consistent effort, I will make it through another day.

LIVING OUT WHAT I SAW

When you are young, your environment can have a major effect on you––positive or negative. You can even acknowledge what is going on around you and think to yourself, *I will not be like that.* I remember saying hundreds of times, "I will never be like my mother." I judged her by how she reacted to situations and said, "I will never act like that." Then years later I found myself reacting the same way! Can you relate to this? I blamed my behavior on Mom as a natural response to mimic the actions I saw.

I also used to say, "I will not turn into my father." Although I do not remember a lot of family drinking when I was young, my mother called Dad an alcoholic. For years I said, "I will not follow in the footsteps of our family alcoholism." I did not choose to become an alcoholic, but I did choose to drink. Because of my decision and the way I drank, I turned into an alcoholic. There is addiction in our family. Several cousins and I are sober today from either alcohol or drugs, and I am proud of them and their recovery journey.

Earlier in the book, I talked about how I banged my head against a wall. That behavior did not just happen to me for no reason. As both a child and adult, I witnessed my mother bang her head against the wall, hit herself in the head with her hands and fists, and bang her head off the car's steering wheel. As crazy as it sounds, I did what I saw. When I felt frustrated or my situation seemed to be out of control, I banged my head against the wall and hit myself with my fists. I gave myself a few concussions over the years, either from the head banging or falling and hitting my head when drunk.

My mother threatened suicide when I was a young, and I believe she was mentally ill to do that. I do not remember the reasons behind her threats, just countless times crying and pleading with her. It instilled fear in my mind, and I carried it throughout my relationships. Many times while driving, she threatened to run us off the road into a tree. As an adult, the thought still comes to my mind, *Just turn the wheel Kelly, and this could all be over.*

I witnessed many blow ups that Mom said stemmed from her being angry with my brother or a fight with my stepfather. I was young and did not understand what was going on. There was yelling, breaking things, turning furniture over, and her hitting my brother and stepfather.

When I was drinking and got into arguments with Tony, I made suicidal comments and threats. I threw objects, broke things, and did exactly what I saw my mother do. I hate that behavior and who I became, but that was the truth of my life then. Since my recovery journey started, I am so grateful nothing like that has happened, and I never have to react insanely again.

I acknowledge those are unhealthy reactions, and I can change the narrative from who I was and who I am becoming. I have learned healthy ways to express my feelings, and it is easier for the person I communicate with to receive them.

As an adult, I have continued to experience suicidal threats from my mother, but my reaction has changed over the years because I have gained some helpful tools. I do not beg her to stop the threats, and I remove my emotions and then call the professionals. I have called them to do wellness checks to make sure she is okay. I have prayed for her and continue to do so with words that say, "God, I pray for You to intervene into Mom's heart. I pray she surrenders and recognizes that her thoughts and actions are not healthy, and she gets help.

We do not have to become a product of our environments and what we saw growing up. We are not responsible for how we were raised, but we are responsible for our future behavior and the relationships that go with them. If we choose to get help, we can change.

When you go through life without being taught healthy behavior, you respond to situations either positively or negatively based on what you have seen modeled. I repeated people pleasing, temper tantrums, fits of rage, physical abuse, and downright hate in my heart. The principles I needed to be taught in my youth to form proper values were not part of my early childhood development, and I have learned to accept that. I do not know much about how my parents were raised, so I believe they just repeated with my brother and me what they saw from their parents.

What happened to me was not my fault, and that took time to process. I now know my future is my responsibility, and I need to heal if I want to have a life of internal peace. Healing is work, and each day I get to work on my new life. I can and have broken my chains, will continue to any time new hurts surface, and move forward with healing as God leads the way.

PART FIVE

LIES THE ENEMY TELLS US

LIES THE ENEMY TELLS US

I have learned that fear is a lie from the enemy, and it seemed I had a million forms of it. At some point, we are all driven by fear. It can show up anywhere, at any time, and can cripple you if you allow it to. Fear can prevent you from asking for and getting help. It terrified me to ask someone for help because it meant I had to be held accountable for admitting I had a problem. If I got the help to quit drinking, I was afraid life would be boring, and I would not have any friends. I also learned that fear can be a choice. I do not want to live in fear, so when it crops up, I must process if it is real or a lie. Most of the time, it is a lie.

I have made some wonderful friends in sobriety, and we have a blast together. Some friends are normal drinkers. I call them "Normies," and I have no problem being around them when they drink. Many of my friends do not drink. I can go out and do the same things I did when I was drinking––minus the alcohol. I do not do bar crawls any longer, and I do not have any desire to.

Dancing is one of my favorite things to do and always has been. I have been out dancing many times sober, and I find myself looking for the drunkest person in the bar and think, *That was me, but I was probably much worse.* It reminds me of how far I have come and makes me grateful for not wanting to be that way anymore. I do not need alcohol to have a good time.

In my former life, I was a gossip queen and surrounded myself with others like me. We would drink all afternoon and talk about people. The gossiping started as early as middle school, and I am not proud of that ugly characteristic. I did not care who or what it was about; if I knew something, I shared it. If I was the person sharing the gossip, I thought I was cool. I did not care about the fallback and repercussions, which was wrong, and I am sure hurtful. As I got older, it became a terrible habit. I felt awful doing it, and then justified my destructive behavior and drank to make the feeling go away. I was fearful of gossip getting back to the person it was about.

I have grown tremendously in this area. I now know what to keep to myself and what can be shared. Not being a gossip was one of my life changes that took practice. Gossip is a slippery slope, and I know staying away from it is a lifelong journey. I must be aware of what is coming out of my mouth before I say it, text it, post it, or type it in an email. I like to use the T.H.I.N.K. acronym. Is it True? Is it Helpful? Is it Informative? Is it Necessary? Is it Kind?

When I am fearful, I ask two questions. "Is this fear coming from *losing* something that I have? Is this fear coming from *not getting* something that I want?" Most likely I am creating the fear in my head, too. It could be a friendship, and I said something to offend them without intentionally meaning harm. It could be a customer's negative review or feedback at work that could cost my business harm. When we first met, I feared losing

Dave when I shared with him about my past. I thought he would judge me and run the other way.

Situations are rarely as bad as you make them out to be in your head. We future trip, become worried and afraid, and then invite God in to help us. God will show us He can help us through whatever we fear, and most of the time we will say, "That was not so bad."

You know what was really frightening? Asking for help. That meant I had to admit my weakness and defeat and that I could not do this on my own. Nobody told me it was okay to ask for help. I thought asking for help made you weak. I felt lonely because I never wanted to tell anyone that I needed help because I would look bad and they would not like me. What a misguided way to think about life.

I did not get help until I met someone that had gone through a similar struggle and shared her experience with me. Since she was open with me, I felt I could tell her what was going on, and that I needed help. I reached out and said, "Please tell me what to do."

I have learned that asking for help is one of the strongest and most courageous steps one can ever take. When you feel weak, God can make you strong. I am so grateful that I know this now and can encourage others to reach out. I hope these two Bible verses about God's strength in our weakness encourage you.

"But he said to me, 'My grace is sufficient for you, for my power is made perfect in weakness.' Therefore, I will boast all the more gladly about my weaknesses, so that Christ's power may rest on me" (2 Corinthians 12:9).

"In the same way, the Spirit helps us in our weakness. We do not know what we ought to pray for, but the Spirit himself intercedes for us with the groans that words cannot express" (Romans 8:26).

When I went through new experiences and new emotions for the first time sober, it was frightening and came with major anxiety. I did not know what to do because I was so used to drinking for every single emotion, birthday, breakup, dreadful day, anniversary, and so on.

When I lived with Amanda and Jay and got my first job offer after moving to Charlotte, I was so excited and immediately started to cry. I did not know how to celebrate without drinking. I felt instantly defeated, began to cry, and then the doorbell rang. Jay returned with a box from UPS with my name on it. It was homemade pumpkin cookies from one of my long-time friends Amy. The card read, "Love you Kel, thinking of you. I hope you love these cookies, my grandmother's special recipe." Alongside the cookies was a book by Renee Swope titled *A Confident Heart: How to Stop Doubting Yourself and Live in the Security of God's Promises*. I looked up to the sky and whispered, "Thank you, God." I knew I was going to be okay. That was a God wink I will always remember.

CRIPPLING FEAR

Crippling fear is the worst for me, and it is created in my mind. I think of something, then choose to dwell on it, become anxious, and then feel overwhelmed with fear. I have a crippling fear of losing my husband Dave. He has been one of my biggest blessings from God, and I can get fearful quickly and create ideas in my mind that I am losing him.

Not long ago I was at the hair salon, and I noticed almost five hours had gone by since I had last heard from Dave via a text or phone call. We talk often throughout the day because of the business or just to say, "Hey, thinking of you." I texted and no response. I called and no response. I called our technician and asked, "Have you heard from Dave?" and he said, "No."

I started to feel anxious, a knot forming in my throat, and lightheaded. My stylist said, "Kelly, what is wrong?" Tears started to well up in my eyes, and I began to panic. I prayed and then my phone rang. It was Dave, and he was fine. He had left his phone on the charger inside the house and was outside with the contractors working on our new garage. The feelings were real, and I feared losing him.

Early in my relationship with Dave, I struggled by believing I did not deserve such a great man. I never had a healthy relationship, and I was waiting for this one to fall apart. Despite looking for things wrong with Dave, I could not find any. I even tried to create faults because I was not used to someone healthy, only dysfunctional or with hang-ups. Dave was patient with me each time I communicated my feelings, and we always talked through my emotions and concerns.

I thank God daily that I get to spend my life with Dave and cherish our time together. I know I must put my trust in God and His plan for my life, especially when I feel afraid.

SCREW FEAR, TAKE THE RISK

Fear can prevent you from going after goals or dreams. If God can put something on your heart, then I believe He already knows you have what it takes to accomplish it. I was fearful of writing this book, started writing, and then stopped for two years because I feared what people would say or think. I started to read Joyce Meyer's book *Do it Afraid* and had not even finished the first chapter when I began to cry because I knew God was speaking to me.

My book is my life and story, and it is meant for someone, but not everyone. Let people talk and judge me. They do not matter. Jesus is the one who saved me, and He approves of me sharing how I went from death to life. Who cares what people will say or think--embrace the goal or dream God has put on your heart and DO IT AFRAID!

I never had a goal or dream to exterminate bugs, but God has a sense of humor! When I met Dave, I had a job in corporate America with good benefits. Dave was in pest control with a big corporation and left to start his own pest business. He was less than two years self-employed, and we were already married, when I took a huge risk and left my job to become a pest technician with him. What in the world was I thinking? He was doing okay financially, but my job included benefits. I thought, *Can we really make it with both of us self-employed and also grow the business?* We did not know, but we took the risk.

I recall being on my knees and crying saying, "Lord, I am so scared, but I trust You will not let us fail. I trust You will take care of us." I knew we could work hard and do our part, but I did not know if the business would sustain our bills. God surely blessed us that first year and again the second year. We give all the glory to God and would not have the business we have today if it were not for taking that risk and stepping out in faith.

This former high school cheer leader went from wearing heels and a dress into an office to wearing work boots and pants outside crawling under houses killing bugs and getting dirty! I still talk to God every time I go into a crawl space and say something like, "Lord, I trust You and know You have a plan for me."

I laugh out loud sometimes when I think about my career. When I first met Dave, I asked him with great curiosity, "People pay you to kill their bugs?" Do it afraid has taken on new meaning for me!

PART SIX

NEW LIFE CONCEPTS

Living In the Solution

If you never learned how to live in the solution, then it makes sense you live in the problem. I did until someone pointed out a new way. For example, I focused on other people's problems and crisis, and stewed and festered about something that had nothing to do with me. Their business became my business and created a mess.

My blood pressure was high and anxiety level extreme. Comments about what I said or did not say replayed in my mind. I future tripped about crazy situations that would likely never happen, and my mind create endless scenarios. I always ended up irritable, restless, and discontent over someone else's life. As you may remember, Jen made an important point when she told me, "That is none of your business. Stay on your side of the street."

Thankfully I know better and if it does not affect me or my immediate family, then I release that person or situation to God and stay out of it. I do not have to be involved in family drama or gossip. What others do and say is none of my business, and not my responsibility. I can detach with love and choose to still love family members, yet never talk to them again, if that is best for me. Setting boundaries is healthy when what someone does and how they live could negatively affect me, my recovery, and my serenity.

Living in the solution is when I say, "I would rather not take part in this conversation" or say nothing at all. No response is a response. Solution living is stating, "This makes me uncomfortable" and then remove myself at any time so I am not part of the problem. God does not want me to engage in other people's business through negativity, gossip, or enabling others with their actions. He wants me to practice love, tolerance, and stay on my side of the street. It goes back to the old saying, "If you don't have anything nice to say, don't say anything at all."

My gossip, criticism, and judgement of others was what I saw growing up. I learned it early and repeated almost everyone else's drama and business. By loving the drama of other people's crisis, I took the focus off how I was living. I put myself in the middle of someone's issue and told them, "This is what you need to do and how to live your life." It was none of my business, especially when someone didn't ask my opinion and I was living incorrectly. I was often right in the middle of the drama and would say, "I dislike like drama" and then gossip and criticize others. I am not proud of how I used to behave.

When I stay out of the chaos, I go to bed with a clear conscious and not lay awake for hours, replaying the insanity of the drama in my head. When I engage, I open myself up to more drama and chaos, and the toxic circle never ends. Constantly staying in the middle of the chaos is not where I want to be anymore. It makes me feel horrible and anxious, and that is not God's will for me.

It sure takes practice to not get involved. I slip up, but get better over time as new situations arise. Progress, not perfection, is an awareness of what I should *not* do and then do it right the next time. I say, "God is testing me to see if I learned from the last time." Sometimes I learn and give myself a pat on the back, and other times I mess up and cringe because I know better. I cannot make the excuse, "I do not know any better" because now I do. Changing old behavior takes time and sometimes longer than one would think. Just keep practicing.

ACCEPTANCE

Acceptance is letting go of what is not in your control. It is an important part of my recovery journey and a frequently continued practice. I cannot control anything except how I react. My reaction can go one of two ways. I can either say things I will regret, or accept whatever it is and move on.

Acceptance is also a choice to acknowledge something as it is. I can choose to reject someone or fight a situation, but my negative attitude and behavior will rule over me and steal my peace. Acceptance in not about agreeing with someone's harmful behavior or a hurtful situation I cannot control. To be healthy, I must accept others for who they are and the journey they are on. I can only change myself, chose what is best, and not focus on what I cannot control.

To practice acceptance, I tell myself, *This situation is supposed to be this way, and if it does not affect me in a harmful way, then I need to move on.* I want to stay focused on solutions for situations I can control, be in the present and not stuck in the past, and enjoy what I have. I want to maintain the serenity I have worked hard for.

HANDLING ANXIETY

Living with anxiety is something I got accustomed to. I thought it was my normal. I learned how to react and took my medication when I was supposed to. If I missed a couple days of taking my pills, I knew life would be emotional hell until I got back on track. The crying and mood swings of highs and lows were such a roller coaster, and I wanted off.

I had accepted anxiety and depression as part of my life, and would always be on medication. Then one day I was in a recovery meeting and heard someone say, "I went off my meds after some time in sobriety." I thought, *I want that!* When I talked to Jen, she directed me to a professional. I made an appointment with my doctor.

I thought, *I never learned what healthy coping was until a few years into being sober. Now I have tools when anxiety creeps up or I know I am going into a situation where I could become anxious. I can use them instead of being medicated.* I shared all this with my doctor and he said, "Let's try it and see how you manage." He suggested weening me off and cut the dosages down a few weeks at a time until I was completely off.

I did this during my last corporate job, and it seemed I used the recovery tools every hour of every day. When a situation came up, I prayed through it. I had breathing exercises and hand movements I practiced to distract me from letting my mind spiral and chest tighten. I talked to God sometimes almost all day just to get through it. The plan lasted a few months, and then I was off medication!

The anxiety did not disappear completely, but I no longer needed the medication. I still have periods of anxiety, but it does not last long. The feeling usually starts when I am about to have an uncomfortable conversation or go into an environment that does not feel like a safe space. I pray and ask God to guide me, and He helps me every single time. Writing this part of the story makes my chest tight and heart race. I breathe deeply and let the Holy Spirit work through me. It may take a minute or up to ten to relax, but I just breathe and pray until I am calm.

About six months after I moved to Charlotte, I volunteered with a pit bull dog rescue and became a foster mom. I decided to not let my tragic experience with Raider, Duke, and Lady stop me from being a passionate pit bull advocate. I wanted to learn from that experience and save more dogs.

I have PTSD when I hear dogs barking or starting to play fight. I become extremely anxious and must remove myself from the situation almost immediately. My nerves are shot at times, but I have done so much work to get better. I fostered many dogs until my current pittie Domino came into my life. He was my foster failure, and I fell deeply head over heels in love with him the few months he was with me.

Today I have two dogs, my pit bull Domino and Hulk, a German shepherd rescue. The two boys are the best of buds. However, when they play fight, I do not allow it to go far because of my anxiety. I do not know if I will carry the PTSD with me forever, but I pray God will continue to protect me and my fur babies from ever having to experience another tragic event. Even after seven years, I cannot unsee and hear what I went through that awful day with Duke, Lady, and Raider.

I am so thankful to be off my anxiety and blood pressure medications. It took plenty of work on my part and wisdom by my doctor. I have learned how to deal with my anxiety and have normal blood pressure. I believe when I stopped drinking and smoking and learned to calm myself, my blood pressure regulated. It took a few years to get to normal, and is a miracle. I continue to pray that my body will heal from all the years I mistreated it.

EXPECTATIONS

When we are young, we have a vision of expectations about our future. The type of job we will have, the family, the marriage partner, the house we live in, and the car we will drive. Then we grow up and the reality of life happens. The delusion of expectations versus what we have is significantly different. We discover our vision is not reality. We are mad, disappointed, and ask ourselves, "Why or how did this happen?" Well, we cannot change the family we have and all the choices we made, but we can change our expectations of ourselves and others.

I used to think that I had to have it all together and tried to come off that way in front of others. The reality was I was not only fooling others, but myself too. I have learned not to expect too much from myself and others. If I do, I set myself up for disappointment. I cannot expect others to understand the journey I am on, and they cannot expect me to understand theirs.

When I moved to the Charlotte area, my dad came to stay with Dave and me for our first visit. I was nervous and wanted our time together to be great. I did not want him to drink, that he liked everything about me and what I was doing, and that we would have the best father/daughter relationship ever. Do you see where my expectations were with this scenario? I was setting myself up for complete disappointment by trying to direct in my head the perfect weekend the way I wanted it to go.

My friend shared with me, "Kelly, have few expectations, take it one hour at a time, and just let the day and weekend happen the way it is meant to." I gave in to her suggestion and let go of control of my dad and our time. We took it one hour at a time during his visit and had a great time. We went to the Nascar race track, played card games, took pictures, went out to eat, he drank a little, and we showed Dad around the area where we lived by the lake. The weekend turned out to be a wonderful memory. Not one bad thing happened, and I surrendered my control and expectations. This mindset and behavior change was an excellent lesson and experience for me.

Gaining Respect

Two weeks into not drinking, I wrote in my journal, "I want to lead a life that gains respect." I had two choices. One was to continue in the wrong steps, which was the life I was living. The second was to learn a new way of life and earn respect. The most important change for me was to respect myself, but I also wanted other people to respect me. I had little regard or esteem for myself, so why would others?

I acted foolish almost every time I drank and just shake my head at the poor choices I made. When someone continues to disappoint you by repeating the same unacceptable behavior, it is easy to lose respect for them. You probably think, *What is the point? They are not changing.*

Over time, by not drinking and putting in the effort to change, I felt proud of myself. When I shared, "I have been two months sober," someone in earlier sobriety was in awe, and that support made me feel good. People cheered me on when I said,

"I have been three months sober," and I loved that feeling of encouragement.

I gain a little more confidence each day when I wake up sober without a hangover. There is a fine line between confidence and arrogance. I am careful not to become too confident and must remain humble because I know if I choose to pick up alcohol, I can spiral out of control.

My long-time friend Amy moved to the Charlotte area when I was a few years sober. I remember the day she asked me, "Will you be my children's emergency contact?" I almost fell over because I went from the "bad influence friend" to the "emergency contact!" It felt good to be trusted. Thank God I have never been called, and will be there sober if I am needed.

Finding someone to love me and respect me is one of the greatest feelings. My confidence has grown because Dave values my opinion and wants to hear what I have to say. Dave honors me by refraining from drinking when he is with me. He does not have a problem with it, nor does he give drinking any value. His actions and beliefs mean the world to me, and God has surely blessed me with this man.

COMPARISON

"Comparison is the thief of joy," Teddy Roosevelt quoted. Do not compare yourself to someone else's journey; it is their journey, not yours. I was very good at comparing myself to others––what they did or had that I did not do or have. Trying to get what others had made me miserable.

A couple of years before I quit drinking, I saw my friend Amy do a bikini fitness competition. I thought she looked amazing, so skinny and fit. My comparison began because we used to party together in college. I thought, *If she can do that, then so can I.* My drinking was affecting my physical appearance, and I was bloated. With an increase in drinking, I was not working out as often as usual.

Comparison led me to do google searches on body building competitions, fitness coaches, and nutrition coaches. I entered a figure body building competition. I had been lifting weights and doing cardio more than half of my life. It made complete sense to me that under all the bloating from alcohol, I had a physically fit body. It was also an opportunity to reduce partying and give myself a break from all the drama and chaos that came along with drinking.

It was ninety days to stage time, and the nutrition coach told me, "Cut out all alcohol." I thought, *Ninety days is doable. I do not have a problem with alcohol.* In that time period, I believed someone my size could drop ten to fifteen pounds and build muscle at the same time. I was in total delusion and complete denial. I could not quit the alcohol no matter how hard I willed it, even if it was just shots of vodka. The obsession to drink was still there despite the desire to do well in the figure competition.

I continued to socialize with friends at the bar, so of course I drank, but not as much. My goal helped with semi-controlled drinking, and I counted down the days until I could drink like I really wanted to.

Stage time came, and I looked amazing. As I got prepared to walk on stage, I wondered, *Imagine if I had done exactly what my coach told me and didn't drink during those ninety days of training?* The thought was dismissed, and I walked out with confidence. I brought my best to the competition––it was not good enough to win, but I placed seventh in my age group. I was happy because I was trying to prove a point to myself that I did not have a problem with alcohol. Surely if I could do training for a competition like that, I was not an alcoholic. Truth was, when I was backstage, I was so nervous that I took shots of tequila to calm my nerves. At intermission I went to the parking lot and smoked pot with some friends that came to cheer me on. *This is totally normal behavior for a normal person,* I told myself.

Despite how great I looked, my mom constantly questioned me throughout my twenties and early thirties about my weight. Finally, I said something that stopped it. I was in my mid-thirties, and it and about a year or two after I quit drinking. Out of frustration from her questions, I said something not too pretty. It was to the point and basically, "What the heck is wrong with you and your obsession about what I weigh and look like? You have given me a body dysmorphia complex for my entire adult life. Leave me alone!" I later apologized for the harsh reaction and explained how harmful her words were to me. I said, "I have had many issues with my body because I learned from you to compare myself to others, especially my weight." Thankfully, Mom never brought it up again.

Comparison kept me from acknowledging for years that I had a drinking problem. I was court ordered when I was twenty-one to attend AA meetings as part of my consequences for a DUI. I remember going into a small building, and walked into a room that had a group of older men chain smoking. My attendance paper got signed, and I do not recall paying attention to what they said. My mind focused on how I looked different from these people and thought, *I am nothing like these people.* I was not open-minded to even consider that I had a problem. I was certainly not ready to hear what I needed and *compared* myself right out of the rooms for the next ten years. My addiction continued to grow and control my life.

I spent time with people that drank like me or much worse. It was easy to compare myself to them and say, "I am not as bad as them" or "I could be much worse." It seemed like I drank normally, like everyone else. People encouraged shots and day drinking, and blackouts were a normal weekend occurrence. We were all unhealthy together, and did not know any different way of life. Every few years, I had a different group of friends. The last group before I quit drinking had several girls who were "normal drinkers" and not alcoholics. When they shared concern about my heavy drinking, I ignored them. I did not know my life would soon change.

When I went back to a recovery meeting eleven years after I quit going, I heard someone say, "Do not compare yourself or you will compare yourself right out of the room." That is exactly what I had done before. They said, "Look for the similarities and stay. You will hear something that is helpful and something that gives you hope. Take what you want and leave the rest." That has helped me in my years in recovery, and I use it in so many areas of life.

In the beginning of my sober journey, I compared myself to other people's recovery journey, which is not healthy. I have learned that everyone does what works for them. There are many ways to get sober. Some people do twelve-step programs or Self-Management and Recovery Training (SMART). Others incorporate counseling. Some start without a recovery program and years later attend one. Other people start with a recovery program, learn the structure and principals, and then stop going. Some use a higher power to get sober.

Just because a certain way works for me does not mean it will work for you. Whatever keeps you from not drinking, who cares how you do it. Just do not drink! What kept me from drinking was I needed everything and anything that was available to help me. I could not do it on my own.

I continually want to grow and do not always know what it looks like. My prayer is, "God, show me how I can become better or grow." He certainly does as I peel back the layers of why I am the way I am and become the healthiest possible version of me. I do not want to compare myself to others because this is my life and journey. I want to be happy with who Kelly is because God created me. Ephesians 2:10 in the Bible says, "For we are God's masterpiece. He has created us anew in Christ Jesus, so we can do the good things He planned for us long ago."

I had to learn to love my body, and get over my body dysmorphia issues and become comfortable in my skin. Weighing myself daily has stopped and my obsession about eating and working out. I learned what healthy eating is and do not feel bad about occasional unhealthy eating and limited sweets.

My work outs help me stay healthy and feel strong. Since Covid hit and the gym closed, I took up running again outside. I found a running buddy who makes the experience much better. Exercise has always been a release, keeps me balanced, and is good for my mental health. I like to say, "I work out to burn off the crazy."

WE ARE CREATED IN GOD'S IMAGE

It took practice to meditate on the scriptures of how God sees me and who I am in Christ. My entire life, I had conflicting negative thoughts of myself. To change this, I recited scriptures over and over, and stood in front of the mirror to read them out loud. I made a choice to believe how God sees me and have learned to love myself how He loves me. I would rather live in God's truth than the enemy's lies.

Because of who I am in Christ, I believe every one of these statements from the Bible to be true. I do not have to worry about comparing myself and my journey to others because my acceptance comes from Christ alone.

I am loved. (1 John 3:3)

I am accepted. (Ephesians 1:6)

I am a child of God. (John 1:12)

I am Jesus' friend. (John 15:14)

I am a joint heir with Jesus, sharing His inheritance with Him. (Romans 8:17

I am united with God and one spirit with Him. (1 Corinthians 6:17)

I am a temple of God. His Spirit and His life live in me. (1 Corinthians 6:19)

I am a member of Christ's body. (1 Corinthians 12:27)

I am redeemed and forgiven. (Colossians 1:14)

I am complete in Jesus Christ. (Colossians 2:10)

I am free from condemnation. (Romans 8:1)

I am a new creation because I am in Christ. (2 Corinthians 5:17)

I am chosen by God, holy and dearly loved. (Colossians 3:12)

I am established, anointed, and sealed by God. (2 Corinthians 1:21)

I do not have a spirit of fear, but of love, power, and a sound mind. (2 Timothy 1:7)

I am God's co-worker. (2 Corinthians 6:1)

I am seated in heavenly places with Christ. (Ephesians 2:6)

I have direct access to God. (Ephesians 2:18)

I am chosen to bear fruit. (John 15:16)

God has given me great and precious promises by which I share His nature. (2 Peter 1:4)

God works in me to help me do the things He wants me to do. (Philippians 2:13)

I can ask God for wisdom, and He will give me what I need. (James 1:5)

Once I repeatedly read and meditated on all these scriptures, I began to believe them. If I focus on believing God's Word (the Bible), there is no more room in my life for comparison. Comparison is a thing of the past, and I have put it to rest.

PEOPLE PLEASING

"Hello, my name is Kelly and I am in recovery from people pleasing." Yes, another thing to add to my laundry list of issues I am recovering from. All I ever wanted was for people to like me and to fit in. I do not recall my mom being a people pleaser, but I wanted to please my mom. I read the Boundaries book by Dr. Townsend, and they talk about when the parent does not get something they want from the child, they withhold love to the child. It hit a cord for me because my mother did that to me and could be where people pleasing developed. I believed they would not like or love me if I did not give others what they wanted. Wherever it came from, people pleasing is an awful way to live, and stole many years of life's enjoyment. For the last couple of years, I have done better to end it.

You can google and take a test "Are you a people pleaser?" I used to check off every bullet on the list. Here are a few examples of how I people pleased throughout my life. *Worrying about what others think about me and what I am doing.* I still sometimes worry if I have upset someone, even when I have no reason to feel that way. *Apologizing for no reason.* When people give me advice, I take their recommendation just to agree with them, even though it may not be the best move.

People pleasing is another area of recovery that when it comes up, I know it is a test. Sometimes I pass and sometimes fail, but I know it will continue to happen and need to be aware of it. God wants me to stop the unhealthy behavior. This stronghold of people pleasing is detrimental to my growth. If I am doing what other people want, then I am not growing towards God's purpose. I need to have my own thoughts and beliefs and stand by them. If people disagree, then that is on them. I know pleasing God is more important than pleasing others, even if they are family or friends. My purpose is to be a great wife to Dave, share Jesus, and help others in recovery or through my daily life.

CHANGING MINDSET

"Therefore, if anyone is in Christ, the new creation has come. The old has gone, the new is here!" (2 Corinthians 5:17)

When I think of this scripture and how it relates to me, I have been given a *do over* at life. About six months after I stopped drinking, I moved to a different state and left everything behind——people, places, and possessions. I had a lot of work to do on myself, and I delayed progress with all the familiar distractions that could tempt me back to drinking. I needed to unlearn everything I thought was true. Throw out the old thinking, the old ways, and completely erase my dysfunctional thinking so I could move forward.

I feel like there were a lot of dysfunctions in my life——mostly self-inflicted——but also from certain friends or family members. Like most people, I learned from what I saw around me. I didn't have a mind of my own and chose what everyone else was doing. It seemed easier to go along with others.

How can you change if you keep doing the same old stuff? Call me crazy, but I still went to the bar several days a week because I knew nothing different. I did this for at least six months before I moved. My routine for years after work and on the weekends was to go to the bar. I did not know there was a very different life waiting for me to find it. I did not realize there were people whose life did not revolve around drinking.

I went to my recovery meetings every day, and some days I went twice when I lived in Virginia. I did not know what else to do. After meetings, I went to the bar and saw my friends. I talked to the bartender about my recovery meetings. They probably thought I was a nut job. How can you go from recovery meeting to the bar? I was asking for trouble by doing this so early in sobriety, and had learned nothing other than to not drink one day at a time. Someone once said, "If you keep going to the barbershop, you will get a haircut." I thought, *How do people live life without drinking?*

After praying for months and not much changing for me, thankfully, God showed up and took over. He answered my prayers when I least expected it. I did a lot of journaling in the first few years of my new life. In one of my journal entries, I wrote all the cities I could move to where I had friends. God put Charlotte, NC, on my heart, and I wrote it down. I had recently changed jobs, so making that list was more of a future dream than anytime soon. The call came in late May on my way home from a weekend visiting friends in Charlotte.

I was an account manager at a staffing company in Virginia, and that had been my career for over ten years. My boss called to give me a heads up. He was resigning the next day because of accepting a new role, and I would not see him in the office. The following day when I got to the office, the boss of my boss called to tell me what I already knew. He said, "Responsibilities will shift in your role, and you will need to go to an all-commission structure or find a new job." Going to all commission was not something that was ever an option. Looking back, this was totally God doing for me what I would not do for myself. I looked up at the sky and said, "Okay God, I hear you!" I would not have left that job to move to another state, but now I had to. This was my chance to leave Virginia and start a new life.

I called my friends Amanda and Jay, who I had just visited that weekend. I asked, "Is the offer to stay with you until I get on my feet serious?"

They said, "Absolutely! Come on down."

I was staying with a couple that opened their home to me when I left Tony six months prior. I said to them, "I am moving to Charlotte" and shared my plan. In four days, I packed up my SUV and left Virginia to move in with Amanda and Jay.

I quickly found a job, and after two months, moved into my own place. The two months with Amanda and Jay had been awesome. I did a lot of journaling, reflecting, and dreaming of a new life. While I lived with them, I had two much needed shoulder surgeries and was very thankful to have them care for me while I recovered. I found meetings close by to attend and started making friends inside and outside recovery. As a volunteer at a Pit bull rescue, I made some great friends to hang out with in my spare time. God was making a way for me.

Romans 12:2 says, "Do not conform to the pattern of this world but be transformed by the renewing of your mind. Then you will be able to test and approve what God's will is—his good, pleasing, and perfect will." That is just what I did. When I moved into my own place, I had more time to myself and to devote to God. I read the *Jesus Calling* devotional and found that I could not just read *one day* at a time, but *many days* in a row and reflect on the scriptures and my life. I was hungry for more and open to receive what God had for me.

I was sober and living alone for the first time in my life. There was a lot of time to read books that fed me with goodness and positivity. I found the books doing a google search of self-help books and asked other people what they liked to read. I searched for Christ-based books because that is what I needed. My focus was on God and what He wanted for my life. I found out that the Bible app has an audible option, and I fell asleep to scripture being read to me.

I never searched for recovery memoirs until I wrote mine. It is exciting to learn about their experience, strength, and hope. I found all kinds of inspiration to follow on social media and books to read to help me with sobriety. My search led me to healing influencers and holistic doctors. I have been working with a trauma therapist to help me process and heal from the pain that resurfaced since I started my memoir. She recommended *brain spotting* as a treatment method, and I have had good results. I love this sobriety journey and am grateful for everyone that has inspired and helped me along the way. I look forward to continued healing, and each day will do whatever it takes to recover.

I love to journal and when I hear or read something that speaks to my soul, I jot it down and read it out loud. I put positive affirmations on post-it notes and placed them in different areas of my apartment to train my brain to think new thoughts. Negative thinking was normal, and I had to force myself to practice new patterns and behaviors. The mentality I live by today is I will do whatever it takes each day to not take a drink. If writing love notes to me on post-it notes helps, then I will continue. To this day, old thinking creeps up, but that happens because I am on a *journey* of change and growth. I am glad that I have the awareness and the tools not to follow for more than a minute or two the negative thoughts.

When you are important to God, Satan will come after you in some way. I have learned that with all of sobriety's blessings comes battles. Expect it and be ready to act. Luke 10:19-20 says, "I have given you authority to trample on snakes and scorpions and to overcome all the power of the enemy; nothing will harm you." What a great promise that is to know that by following Jesus, I can choose not to let the enemy harm me.

There is that word again, *choice*. I do not have to stay with a thought any longer than as quickly as it comes into my mind. I can redirect my mind to something else. Typically, I pray or call a girlfriend or Dave to share where my head is at. I sometimes turn on worship music and drown out the negative thoughts. There are so many tools to choose to use instead of wallowing in the negative cesspool of lies the enemy wants you to hear. Take back your mind. It belongs to you and no one else. You are the author of your story.

You must retrain your brain to think new thoughts, new patterns, and a new way of life. One of my favorite quotes by Thomas Jefferson is, "If you want something you've never had, you must be willing to do something you've never done." You must have that *whatever it takes* mentality so that when you are broken, do not want to be stuck anymore, and find yourself at your rock bottom––doing something *different* is easier than staying the same. Change is difficult and uncomfortable, but necessary for a healthy life.

Where do you find a new way of thinking if your normal behavior is negativity, over-reacting, unrealistic expectations, name calling, etc.? You must figure out what works best for you. The answer is not one dimensional, and there are a variety of ways. I found it with God being first, self-help books, counseling, and recovery meetings. As I mentioned earlier...take what you want, leave the rest, and do that.

How do I know what is good verses bad thinking? I ask myself, *Does it align with what God thinks about His children? Does the thought go toward God or away from Him?* I do not believe that God ever has horrible thoughts about me. He felt sad by the actions and choices I made in the past and disappointed by mistakes I make now. I absolutely believe that God loves me and He loves you.

If I have a negative thought, that is not from God. I used to think horrible things about myself. When I first got sober, I went into an outpatient facility and given a list of positive quotes from famous people. They asked us to choose which ones related to us. I could not find any to identify with and took all the positive quotes and made them negative about myself. That is how screwed up my thinking was!

How did I get to this point of self-criticism? From years of going down the same negative path. I had to create a new one. There is an analogy in one of my favorite discipleship studies, [1]*Keys to Freedom*, that I cannot get out of my head because it is so true. "The only way to re-direct our thoughts is to stop walking down the old thought trails and choose to create new ones

---

[1] *Keys to Freedom* link is https://mercymultiplied.com/keys-to-freedom-study/

that take us in a different direction." *Keys to Freedom* is an eight-week study designed to equip people of all ages to LIVE FREE and STAY FREE!

Isn't that what I want? To live free and stay free? Create new thought patterns? When I know it is Satan putting negativity in my mind, I rebuke the thought in Jesus' name. I say out loud, "Get out!" It takes time, practice, and being in God's Word to develop this habit. This may sound a little silly saying it out loud, but it becomes a new habit. I would much rather sound silly forming this habit than having an addiction.

Power is knowing foremost who you are in Christ. You can reject anything if you do not want it. Speaking God's words over myself was a good place to start, and the post-it notes in my apartment helped tremendously. I no longer live there, but I still have index cards of scripture and post-it notes on the wall in my home office.

There is nothing sadder than to hear someone in my small group talk down about herself. She is no different from how I was when I entered outpatient rehab. I listen to her share and then say, "I can relate" and share an experience I had. I talk about what God thinks of her, that it is a process to grow through, and it takes time and effort. My reminder is always, "You are never alone and do not have to go through life alone." The Bible tells us, "Two people are better off than one, for they can help each other succeed. If one person falls, the other can reach out and help. But someone who falls alone is in real trouble" (Ecclesiastes 4:9-10).

When you learn *who* you are in Christ and *whose* you are, things change. You get a new attitude. You walk a little lighter and hold your head a little higher. Remember, it does not happen overnight, but it does happen if you do the work. You must keep walking down those new trails.

Another lesson I learned when I sat in recovery meetings day after day and year after year was who I wanted to be around. I liked people who pointed me toward the solution to my issues. The answers for me are in one of a two books——The Bible and the Twelve-Steps *Alcoholics Anonymous* recovery book. When I find myself squirrelly, irritable, or discontent, I go to one of the two books for my solution. It is that simple for me. I usually call a friend or my sponsor Jen. It is always a good idea to bounce an idea off another person to get a different perspective. I must be careful not to call too many people because that is looking for the answer I want to hear and not the solution. Sometimes the solution is I need to be called out because my thinking is flawed. As I take action on the answers I need for my attitude or situation, the more growth and change I experience.

PART SEVEN

FINDING FREEDOM

FORGIVENESS

Forgiveness means to pardon the offender for what they did intentionally or unintentionally. Forgiveness never crossed my mind until I got into recovery. Why on earth would I forgive people who hurt me, especially intentionally? Forgiveness was something I worked on and suddenly made sense. It is another *choice* we get to make. You choose whether or not to forgive. Forgiveness seems so much more complicated than that, but it is not. If we do not choose to forgive the people that have hurt us, then we cannot truly be free. When you forgive someone, you are set free from the bondage of holding onto the hurt. When we choose not to forgive, we stop our progress and the purpose God has called us to. Unforgiveness leads to resentment, and if you stay stuck in resentment, it becomes a chain that holds you back.

I had a tough time at first forgiving the men who molested me. How could I forgive that? I was an innocent child. Then I went to the Bible to learn about forgiveness. "For if you forgive other people when they sin against you, your heavenly Father will also forgive you. But if you do not forgive others their sins, your father will not forgive your sins" (Matthew 6:14-15). "Do not judge, and you will not be judged. Do not condemn, and you will not be condemned. Forgive, and you will be forgiven" (Luke 6:37). "And when you stand praying, if you hold anything against anyone, forgive them, so that your Father in heaven may forgive you your sins" (Mark 11:25).

I want to please my heavenly Father, so today I choose to forgive. I had to let go of the anger I held onto and release to God what my offenders did and deal with them. It does not mean that what they did was right. For me to live freely, I had to forgive and move on. I have learned that hurt people hurt people. My offenders most likely had themselves been hurt in some way. Whether or not they had, I did not want to be tied down any longer to hate and resentment.

I never knew how strong I was until I had to forgive someone who was not sorry for their actions. Sometimes people are so sick in their own way that they do not understand what they do hurts people. Forgiveness is not done to benefit others; it is to set us free from the bondage unforgiveness holds on us.

I also had to forgive myself. There was a lot of anger I had toward myself. I used to think, *How could I be so stupid? What an idiot I am!* I had very little self-respect. I hurt many people and did a lot of damage to my spiritual self, my mind, and my body. I had to forgive myself for not knowing better, giving others power over me, past behaviors, and for the survival patterns and traits I developed during the trauma.

MAKING AMENDS

I never heard the words "making amends" until I was working through the twelve steps. What it meant was I had to own up to my part in doing wrong to others for as far back as I could remember. That was a lot of people. Apologizing was not very difficult for me because I am pretty good about it. "I am sorry" was a part of my everyday vocabulary, and I said it often but not with good motives. Most of the time was to get off the hook for something, and I said it, but did not mean it.

I have learned that apologizing without change is just manipulation. Saying "I am sorry" and verbalizing out loud what I did wrong was difficult. It was necessary to make amends for the lying, cheating, embarrassing times, and putting people in scary situations and uncomfortable scenarios. I got knots in my throat apologizing to some people because it was uncomfortable to say what I did. A lot of my amends were admitting to being sick and selfish because that was my reality.

I made a list of people to apologize to––even those I did not want to or did not think deserved it. The first list was very long, and I went through it one person at a time. I wrote what I did and called or met them in person to apologize. I asked God to help me with the words, and sometimes I bounced my thoughts off another person. Role playing what I was going to say helped because I was nervous and scared.

I wanted to be free from the past and move on with a clean slate. I had to take responsibility for my actions repeatedly with people in my life to make things right, and I was okay with doing it. Thankfully, no one responded negatively. There were people who never spoke to me again, but that was something I needed to be okay with. Even though I apologized, some people wanted to see long-term changes, which is their choice.

When I made amends to Tony, I had to go into it with pure intentions and the right motive. It was about me acknowledging what I did and my part. I apologized for what I did wrong and owned up to it. The amends went better than expected. Tony received it well and said, "I am happy you are doing better." He never apologized, and that is something I had to accept. My motives were pure, and the amends were about me, not him. I could not expect something in return for doing what was right for me. My journey is growth and focus on healing from my issues and not to worry about what other people do that is none of my business.

Years ago when I was drinking, most nights I blacked out or passed out. The nights I was awake, I laid in bed with worry and anxiety about the drama and chaos in my life. Now that I am sober and continue working through recovery, I go to bed with a clear conscious. Over the last few years, I have not had to make many amends. I try to live right and not hurt others. Sometimes it happens, and I own up to it right away, or a day or two goes by and realize that I need to apologize.

If I lie awake at night thinking about a situation more than I should be, it means God has put someone on my heart, and it is an opportunity to act, perhaps with amends. Some people I had forgotten about or did not think I owed them an amends. Over the years, when they popped into my head, I prayed on it, got in touch with them, or looked them up on social media and reached out. There is one person I have been praying about for years, and I cannot find her. I hurt her when I was a teenager before I even drank. I would love to apologize to her and pray that God presents the opportunity when the time is right. He knows my heart and if that will ever happen. In the meantime, I live free through forgiveness of others and myself, and I sleep better by taking action on my amends.

AWARENESS

I now realize that self-awareness is an ongoing process. Having a clear mind and being able to process life as it comes has been such an adventure each day. I choose to look at life from a different perspective now, and it has made all the difference. With the blessings come the battles, because that is how life goes. You must take the good with the bad. The awareness and tools I have today to manage my life is what I believe healthy looks like. A healthy mind is everything to me, and I am grateful to wake up and thank God for another day.

Nobody knows exactly what will happen today or tomorrow. What I know is if I take care of myself as best as I understand how to, that is good enough. I focus on what I can do today and not worry about what happened in the past or fret about the future. This mindset was not something I gained overnight and had to be taught what healthy looks like. I struggle at times, and that is okay, too. I will continue to do my best, and that is all that matters to me. When I stumble and fall, which I know will happen, I will get back up. Sometimes I future trip, see the spiral start, and then I use the tools that work for me. I pray out loud, get on my knees, turn on worship music, pull out my Bible, call my husband, or call a friend. I know what I need to do when the spiral starts.

I had to listen to other people's experiences and their suggestions about what worked for them. I listened to hundreds of sermons from different pastors and went to speaker meetings for various programs. Podcasts and YouTube videos are helpful of other women who have shared their experience. I read different self-help and Christian books. I take what God puts on my heart and want to use it in my own life. Not everything others do will be right for me, and that is okay. Not everything I do will be right for others. All that matters is we keep moving forward toward our goal. My goal is healthy relationships, peace of mind, and serenity. What does your goal look like?

I know Jesus loves me, and He wants nothing but blessings over my life. What I must do each day is focus on how God wants me to grow. I knew I was maturing when I learned every situation does not need a reaction. My reactions in the past were all self-driven, and my motives were wrong. I made most situations about myself and what I wanted rather than think, *How can I be of service to others and God today?* I had to understand that the world does not revolve around me. Imagine that?! I had skewed and delusional thinking.

My recovery has included awareness of thinking I am doing something good but with wrong motives. I met a girl who was in early sobriety living in her car. I told her she could stay with me on my couch. After about a week, I got annoyed because she appeared to be lying around all day doing nothing. I thought, *She should be out looking for a job and going to meetings to help herself.* This is when awareness became important. I allowed her to stay with me––good motive––but I expected her to do what I thought she should do––wrong motive. This was mind altering for me and a great lesson. I invited her to my house, and she accepted. I am grateful for the opportunity to have walked through this experience and learned whatever I do should be with the right motive and no expectations.

Have you ever been around a situation that does not involve you, but you walked right into it and acted like you could take control? You tell others your thoughts and believe they should just stop what they are doing and listen to you? That was me. I must really practice restraining my tongue when I have conversations to not impose my thoughts and will unless asked. My place is to listen and only share when asked my thoughts and advice. I can talk about my experience and what works for me, but never impose what I think others should do. Be like a consultant who provides options and lets people make their own choices. It is their life, not mine.

There is power knowing you do not have to engage in or react to anything you do not want to. It is freeing to know that other people's lives--how they think and act--have zero to do with me. Awareness of what others do or go through is their business and none of mine. I do not have to take on someone else's situation or drama just because I know them, especially family. It is very difficult for me, and I continue to ask God for help in this area of my life. I struggle to let family make their own choice that may not be God's will. I need to stay on my side of the street and mind my own business. All I know to do is pray for them and be a good example.

Social media can be a dangerous place for some people, and here is where many tests or fumbles have had negative outcomes for me. For instance, when someone puts a comment out on social media and I know it is to bait others into an agreement or disagreement, I do not have to engage. I can mind my business and keep scrolling. Many times I made the mistake of posting a comment, someone disagrees with me, and all hell breaks loose. I tell myself, *Okay Kelly, do not engage next time. Learn from your fumbles!* People often post to get affirmation, and if you disagree, you better be ready to argue. Awareness is to think it through knowing, "If I comment, it could take me down a negative path, so do not even go there." Everything is a choice, and I can play the tape out in my head and not chose anything that is negative for my mental health.

My mental health is very important, and I must take care of and protect it at all costs. I must fill my head with positive thoughts and think about the good things that I have. I used to suffer from never being satisfied. It is an ugly way to live. I was rarely happy with what I had and always wanted more, more, more, and what everyone else had.

Today, I supply my head and soul with God's truth. He could only fill the giant-sized hole in my life. Finding gratitude in life instead of what I do not have has been a game changer. Every day I write or say out loud five things I am grateful for. Someone shared that principle with me, and I love to share it when a friend is in a negative spiral. Focus on what you have.

I also dwelled far too long on the negative and on what could go wrong. As a teenager, I would tailspin in negativity and fear that my anxiety would cause ulcers. My stomach always seemed to be upset. I allowed the devil to tell me lies about myself and believed them. Now that I know better, I believe the devil was also feeding my mother lies that she believed.

My awareness now is to know in my heart and head when a negative thought comes in, it is a lie from Satan. Just because you follow God does not mean you stop having negative thoughts. I still get them and say out loud, "Go away, Satan."

Satan uses any small opening in your day to slip a lie into your mind, and he will do it when your guard is down and you least expect it. He will do it when you doubt yourself in the middle of making a decision. Satan tries it when something good happens in my life. He says, "Kelly, you do not deserve that." I know it is a lie! The Bible tells us, "The thief comes only to steal and kill and destroy; I came so that they would have life, and have it abundantly" (John 10:10). "All praise to God, the Father of our Lord Jesus Christ, who has blessed us with every spiritual blessing in the heavenly realms because we are united with Christ" (Ephesians 1:3).

Knowing God's truth and that He wants nothing but goodness for me and my life tells me I can rise and find the strength to choose not to wallow in the negative thoughts and cast out whatever lie the enemy tries to push on me. Just because I did not have the best beginning of my life does not mean I will not have a great ending.

I have learned that we do not have to live out becoming a product of our environment. We must acknowledge, "This cannot be normal. My thinking and way of life is wrong and not healthy, and I need to find a better way. I can change the path I am on anytime. It is never too late to change. I am not too broken for God to work a miracle in my life." Identify that you are the author of your own story and write the ending differently!

WHAT IS A GOOD CHOICE?

Joyce Meyer wrote in her book *Do it Afraid* "If you ever want to make good decisions, stop saying you have trouble doing it. Start declaring that you believe you hear God's voice clearly and that you are able to make good decisions."

Making good choices was something I never did well. Just look at my track record. It took a lot of bad decisions for me to get to the good ones because I am stubborn. If I was hit over the head with a good decision, I pushed it away because I was comfortable making bad decisions. I felt normal in dysfunctional relationships because that is all I knew. Selfishness drove my decisions, and I lived in what was easier in the moment or what someone else wanted me to choose.

Today I know what making good choices looks like. It took a lot of practice. Practice does not necessarily make perfect, but it does make progress. I had to learn to stop and pray––to pause before anything else and add the prayer in. Pausing also took practice because I often reacted without thinking something through. My normal response was what I thought another person wanted and rarely wondered, *What do I want?* I was all about the people pleasing or self-gratification. Never did I ask myself, *What is God's will for me?*

Making choices now seems simple to me, but can still be a challenge. Even in big decisions, like quitting a job, I think, *Is this going toward God's will or away from His will?* My way of thinking changed a few years ago, and I started making better choices. Life became less drama and chaos because those coincide with bad choices. With drama and chaos comes guilt, remorse, and shame. All these negative feelings happen when I do not consider God's will, so now I pause and pray.

God usually shows me a roadblock or a red flag if it is not His will. I must pay attention and be aware of what He reveals to me. "Thy will be done" is what I need to remind myself––not Kelly's will. God wants His best for me and my life. He also wants me to avoid bad choices and hurtful situations.

God does not want me to be a drunk and use alcohol to cope with everyday life.

God does not want me to be in an open marriage, sharing myself with others.

God does not want me to be with someone who uses my past against me.

God does not want me to use my body to feel love and attention from others.

God does not want me to allow others to cross my physical and emotional boundaries.

God does not want me to inflict emotional and physical pain on myself.

God does not want me to engage in toxic relationships, whether it be friends or family.

God does not want me to feel guilty about setting boundaries with others.

God does not want me to think or talk badly about myself.

KELLY STAIB

This list is a lot longer than what I used to think was okay and engaged in, but today I know they were not good decisions for my life. My belief was, "I will never recover from all the shame," but I now know the Bible says, "With God all things are possible" (Matthew 19:26).

I remember vividly when Dave and I started to date again, I prayed daily and multiple times throughout the day. "God, please show me any red flags with this man. I want the man you want for me." I was adamant about making a good decision and needed God's help. His timing is always perfect. In premarital counseling with Dave, I told my pastor, "Find something wrong with him." When nothing surfaced, I knew I was living in God's will with Dave. God made it so easy and effortless to be with this man. It makes me happy to know that I surrendered our relationship to God before marrying him. We both surrendered our will, and God has immensely blessed this union.

LIFESTYLE CHOICES—LOOKING BACK

Participating in an open relationship was a choice I made that was so far from God's will in my life. I had to experience it and get on the other side to realize this bad choice was not in alignment with God's intention for me. I was living in my will and in the moment and did not think of the repercussions that

134

could unfold. Looking back, I am not proud of what I did and how I behaved, but it happened and is part of my story.

One person asked me, "I can tell you do not want to do this, so why do you?" Working on the root of why I chose that lifestyle was simple. My motives were wrong. I got showered with attention, even if it was the wrong kind, and it made me feel special at the moment. I forced myself to be a part of it because I felt included and liked––always seeking affirmation, acceptance, and happiness through others. Even after I got it, I still had an emptiness inside. There was a hole in my soul that only God could fill. I was never satisfied, and nothing ever seemed good enough. I always found something wrong with what I did, and I knew in my heart my behavior was wrong for me. To engage in the actual act, I almost always had to be on something.

When I stopped drinking and was learning to make better choices, I wanted to see if I could do this lifestyle sober. I went to a couple parties but quickly realized, being sober-minded, that it was not for me and would never happen again. I shut the door on that part of my life. Part of my recovery journey has been to figure out what works and what does not work for me in my new life.

I do not regret the experience because I met some good people along the way and am still friends with some of them. I believe God put people in my path during that season that I later needed in my life. One person planted the seed of sobriety for me. I met her on vacation, and we stayed in touch over the years.

She was one of the first people to tell me, "Get your butt to a recovery meeting." I called her, devastated about where I was in life and needed help. She was the shining light in the darkness. God sent her, and I am forever grateful.

I hope sharing my experience will help someone. I gave it all to God and do not have to carry the burden and shame any longer. Early on when we dated, I shared it with Dave because I wanted him to know, "This will never happen in our relationship and marriage. I want you to want me, and me only." I was told that every man wanted to be with other women. Dave made it very clear, "That is not true and not every man thinks that way, especially me."

It is nice to talk and be honest with Dave about my past and receive no condemnation or judgement. I have done some crazy things and did not scare him away. After dating men that did not work out, I realized qualities I needed in a partner and found them in Dave. He loves me for the woman I have become and continue to work toward every day. Our relationship is the opposite of every one I have ever had. God blessed me with Dave, and every day I am thankful.

In past relationships, I wanted to be married to someone that was a believer, and I have that today. God is at the forefront of our marriage, and that is such a blessing I cherish and do not take for granted. We pray together, talk about our plans, and how we are grateful for all that God has provided in our life, family, and business.

PROGRESS

"Progress in your journey one trial at a time."

--Kelly Staib

The first couple of years being sober I heard many times, "You are right where you are supposed to be." I had so much work to do on myself and believe some days I still do. My personal journey is unique and has unfolded the way it is meant to. My growth is my effort on God's timeline, and I want to remain teachable. I will because I want to please my Father in heaven.

I realize mistakes are a part of life. I can go through my day and then--*bam*--I make a mistake. It is okay if you trip up. Give yourself grace and move on. I do not beat myself up anymore because I understand I will never be perfect, nor do I want to be. Jesus is perfection, and He is all I need to help me through. Now I acknowledge what happened, make it right, and make a plan for the next time that situation comes around.

Taking a *daily inventory* is something I do. What is a daily inventory? I learned in recovery to reflect and ask myself questions throughout the day or week such as, *Have I wronged anyone? Have I done something I should not be doing? Have I been dishonest? Did I act inappropriately?* I cannot go to sleep at night knowing that day I did not live right. When occasionally the answer is "Yes," it is not much to worry about, but I want nothing on my conscience that day. I want to be free from everything that holds me back from my purpose.

Rejection/Abandonment

Your loved ones may abandon you, but it has nothing to do with you. I went through most of my youth and adult life carrying a heavy burden of rejection and abandonment that was not mine to carry. God wants us to give Him our burdens so that He can carry them for us. I wrongly focused on the people that could not give me what I longed for. What others do is their life and their choice. It is what is going on inside them, and they will have to deal with the consequences. Some people are not capable of what I need them to be, and I had to accept that. It was a new principle that had to be explained to me, and I had to understand it and be okay with the outcome.

You know what was hard to acknowledge? People will not like me. Ugh, that was a dagger in my heart and asked myself, *What did I do wrong for that to be reality?* It is simply life, and I need to accept it and move on. Focus on the people that love you. Focus on how God sees you.

I learned in recovery that not everyone will support you as you take steps to change, and that is okay. Some people, for various reasons, want you to fail. That has nothing to do with you. Some friends will not support your success, and that is okay. Remember, what other people think is none of your business, so work on yourself and not worry about them. This is your journey, and it is best to follow God's plan and please Him. "For God is working in you, giving you the desire and the power to do what pleases him" (Philippians 2:13).

TRAUMA BONDING

For over twenty-five years, my relationship with my mother has struggled. I have wanted, hoped, and prayed for something different from I have experienced. The reality of our relationship has been so far from what I yearned for between a mother and daughter. I learned in my journey that what I experienced and the way I responded to my mother, brother, and one of my sexual abusers was that I was trauma bonded to them.

According to [2] *The Betrayal Bond* by Patrick Carnes, who developed this concept, "trauma bonds are the dysfunctional attachments that occur in the presence of danger, shame, or exploitation. Trauma bonds occur when we are bonding to the very person who is the source of danger, fear, and exploitation." Here are some signs of trauma bonding Carnes talks about that I have experienced.

- You continue to be fixated on people who hurt you and who are no longer in your life.

---

[2] *The Betrayal Bond* by Patrick Carnes

- You crave contact with someone who has hurt you and who you know will cause you more pain.

- You continue to revolve around people who you know are taking advantage of you or exploiting you.

- You are committed to remaining loyal to someone who has betrayed you, even though their actions indicate few signs of change.

- You are desperate to be understood, validated, or needed by those who have indicated they do not care about you.

- You go to great lengths to continue to help, caretaker, or consider people who have been destructive to you.

I lived all this for so many years and stuck in a sick, unhealthy mental space. I did not realize the depth of my trauma until I was in the middle of writing this book. A counselor helped me process this new information and work through it. My writing has uncovered areas I need to continue to work on, and I am committed to becoming the woman God created me to be. I will make mistakes and learn and will continue my progress to do better and triumph. I owe it to the scared little girl that I was all my life who is now breaking free. There is so much freedom in growth.

TOXICITY/BOUNDARIES IN RELATIONSHIPS

My mental health is especially important to me, and I must take care of it and protect it at all costs today. That means if people, places, and situations are harmful to it and/or recovery, I will take appropriate action to avoid or end it. I can end friendships and relationships. I can cut off family members and quit jobs. If anything at all compromises my serenity and mental health, it must go. I did not work hard these past years to go backwards in my growth, and I will not do it. Some relationships go quickly and others slowly, but the unhealthy ones have always found their way to some sort of end. Certain relationships have been more challenging to terminate.

Toxic people or boundary-crossing individuals usually come with red flags, and until a few years ago I typically ignored red flags. I used to think, *Any friends are better than no friends,* and thought the same with family and relationships. When I brushed the red flags under the rug, I later resented people when it was my fault for staying in the relationship. I expected them to change, and they did not. My expectations of some people and relationships were way off base. Those people were not capable of growth, change, or getting honest with themselves. That certainty was something difficult for me to grasp. I get it today and understand it, but I had to walk through the disappointment and in some sense relationship failure.

I believed I could fix people to make them what I wanted them to be. That attitude is laughable and wrong, looking back at it. I thought, *If they love me enough, they will change.* Changing someone else that does not see a problem with themselves is far from reality in my experience. The only person I can change is me—so with hard work and God's help, I did it.

It is easier now for me to know and recognize what is toxic behavior or people trying to cross my boundaries. The red flags jump out and alert me, so I can process and determine my next step.

I get a physical gut feeling inside—that I know is the Holy Spirit—that lets me know this person, place, or situation is not for me. When I feel like I am walking on eggshells, that is always a surefire sign of toxicity. If I feel fear or impending doom, I need to quickly escape the situation. When I curb how I talk or deliver a message to help a person hear something I want to say, that is okay. If I *compromise* who I am to make them comfortable, that is not okay. I know that my serenity is in jeopardy and need to produce a plan to escape.

Whether it be a family member, a relationship, a friendship, or a job, I used to stay in toxic situations because I was afraid of what others thought and would say about me and my actions. I compromised my happiness to please others, even when it hurt me. I worried about others and did not take care of myself first. These are all traits of being codependent. I never heard the word codependency until I went to Celebrate Recovery—a Christian-based program that helps you heal from your hurts, habits, and hang-ups. In addition to attending that meeting, I researched and watched videos to understand more and learn how to overcome codependency. Unfortunately, it is not like a light switch you just turn off. Freedom comes with an awareness of your behavior, the situation, and a lot of practice.

The first toxic relationship I left was my marriage. Wow, that was a hard one. I was scared to death, but it had to go. I left Tony because of a variety of reasons, but mainly because we were not healthy together. The only foundation of our marriage was partying. I could not remain sober in that environment because I did not get the support and encouragement I needed, probably because of our lifestyle and the years of abuse I put Tony through. I am grateful for the people who were there for me and were exactly what I needed during those early months.

In my heart, I knew the marriage would not work because of the choices and damage we had both done. I was tired of my crap and his crap. I wanted Tony to change, and he did not think there was anything wrong. He wanted me to change, and that got us nowhere. It was a genuine struggle for me to realize that I cannot change others, no matter how much I wanted it. My codependency was prominent, and the only person I could change is myself--and I did just that.

I was told early in sobriety to change anything that compromised my sobriety. People, places, and situations needed to change. I was also told not to make any drastic changes like getting a divorce. However, I left my marriage close to a month of being sober. Leaving a codependent relationship is difficult, and the struggle was real for me. In the end, we were not compatible, and that is okay. I wished Tony well and meant it, and I have often prayed for blessings to go his way. My first marriage was a chapter of my life I do not regret because it made me who I am today.

I never knew what I truly wanted in a relationship until after I left and worked on myself. I figured out who I was becoming, what I wanted, and what I deserved. God revealed to me over time all that He wanted me to know and have.

Thankfully, with a lot of help from God and the people and resources in my life, I continue to cross off the codependent traits. It took years to become codependent, and I am sure it will take time to become healthy and reclaim the life God has planned for me.

Family is a challenge when protecting my mental health, guarding sobriety, and ending a relationship. It is a current struggle as I write this book. I have family members with untreated alcoholism and mental health issues who do not see they have a problem. They continue to stay stuck and not get help. If I engage with them in a conversation, it always goes south as soon as I set my boundaries and stand firm in my beliefs. It hurts and brings me pain and heartache to see them trapped, but I get it because at one time, that was me.

I have learned that you cannot get better in sick environments. I had to move out of the state to get better. Staying around family restricted me from fulfilling God's purpose in my life. I do not believe I could have grown and healed if I had stayed in Virginia. I needed distance to allow God to work in and through me, and He certainly has.

Being open to receive help with my healing journey has continued to open more doors to areas I need to grow in or people I need boundaries with. I asked God for several years, "Help me with my relationship with my mother." He showed me what I needed to know through other people sharing experiences with their family. I am not an expert in psychology but could identify similar patterns and behaviors I have experienced with my mother.

I figured out that our relationship is unhealthy. Every time I talk to her, I feel hurt and confused, and when I get off the phone am mad at myself for repeating the same behavior that upsets me. When it continues to hurt me more than help my healing journey, I must let it go. Breaking off our relationship does not mean forever, but will be for this season however long it takes.

A person with healthy boundaries would probably say, "Stop engaging and detach with love. You can honor your family and love them from afar or with brief communication. Stop answering their calls and do not reply to their text messages." It is easier said than done, especially with my history. I still have some codependency issues, and setting boundaries with family has been difficult, but I continue to work on it. I have ended relationships with a few people and been able to stop going back to the place where I get upset every time that I engage with them. This is another choice I have made.

God wants me to have healthy boundaries and not allow people to cross them. It wasn't until I was thirty-five years old that I learned about boundaries. I never knew *how* to say no or that I *could* say no. I learned that my personal space was mine, and it was not okay if I did not invite someone into it. So much regret and shame came out of not being able to say no, not pushing someone away, and letting them take advantage of me without saying a word. I was afraid of what could happen if I said, "I do not want to go through with this."

Over the years, I allowed people to have their way with me, and I let it happen even if I did not want to take part. This repeated promiscuity through college and in an open marriage made me hate myself. I did not know how to do anything about it but drink and hate my life more and more. And drink I did.

The first couple years of being sober and single, I did not fully focus on my recovery from alcohol and dysfunctional behavior. I also multi-tasked with dating. The "perfect recovery" for me would have been not to date, but I often learn the hard way. I wanted to pay attention this time to all the red flags that were unhealthy for me. There were a lot of first dates and some second dates with different men. I went out with them until I found something wrong, or a red flag smacked me in the face, and then moved on.

You may remember I briefly dated Dave because he could not have any more children, and I wanted to have a child. We remained friends and still occasionally talked. Being Dave's friend, I felt comfortable being honest and sharing the not so pretty facts about my life because I knew we were just going to be friends. I assumed anyone that knew the real me and my past would never be capable of loving me. Who could see past all my years of horrible decisions?

Dave was a good listener and did not pass judgment on me. I called him one night after I failed miserably at keeping a boundary I set with a man. The guy pushed himself on me after I told him, "I was not interested in anything more than getting to know you." How did I get here again?

Dave explained something I had never heard before that was so profound, I will never forget it. He said, "Kelly, you have a voice. You get to say 'No' out loud and not just in your head. Your body is your temple, so protect it." I gained a lot of respect for Dave that day.

I have worked on boundaries for a few years and will continue to do it. I am better than when I started, but still not great. God often provides little boundary tests for me, and I frequently fail. I usually cry and then call a friend or talk to Dave about what happened, what I said, and then what I should say for the next time. I spent most of my life with poor boundaries, and it will take a lot of time to get better with them.

Despite what people may think, healthy boundaries are not created to hurt others. The purpose is to protect yourself from whatever you decide is important. In my experience, the people that get upset with me setting boundaries are the ones that have an agenda and try to cross them. Boundaries are usually more difficult when it is family. Blood is <u>not</u> thicker than peace. If the relationship does not help you move toward peace and happiness, let it go.

Toxic Work Environments

I have been in a handful of toxic situations in my career. The one that stands out the most was my last role before I left corporate America. It was the throw my hands up in the air and say, "It would be easier to change careers than stay in this toxic environment." I honestly believe God put me in that role for my exact purpose, and He orchestrated every step of that season for His purpose.

Dave and I were already married about a year, and I was working on my inner self and seeing lots of growth. My job role started out great, and then my customer hired a man I had to work for. I invited God into conversations with this man because I could not do it alone. His expectations and demands were ridiculous, and everything was a fire. There was no room for any mistakes, and if someone on my team messed up, I had to fire them. I was constantly hiring and firing that year. It was so stressful. My team disliked him, and so did I.

It got to where there was no winning with him, and I felt very frustrated. No matter what I did or how hard I worked, he always found something to disagree with or point out what was wrong or not the way he wanted it. I needed guidance and courage to get the heck out of there. Once again, here is where God did for me what I could not do for myself.

The job provided a good salary and title that I had always been working toward, and yet I was miserable. I worked ten, twelve, and sometimes sixteen-hour days and still feared it was not hard enough. I even took my work on my honeymoon out of fear I would get in trouble if I did not return emails and keep up with assigned tasks. There was so much fear and anxiety in this role. Within a little over a year, the man asked that I be removed from the team, and I knew he did not want me there.

I came to a crossroads and needed to make a choice. I could continue to interview for similar roles in the corporate world and take a chance of finding myself in a comparable situation at the next place. The other choice was to join Dave in his quickly growing pest control business. I thought, *Seriously, God? You want me in pest control? What does that look like? I'm used to heels and a dress. There is no guaranteed salary, and what does 'pay myself' even look like? I have never done this before. How will we be able to afford our bills and independent health care?* So many questions were circling in my mind.

I have learned that what I am supposed to do is invite God into every aspect of my life. Let God lead the way, even when I am terrified, and do it afraid. I need to trust His will and that He will take care of me. Trust God even when I am scared, and I did just that. I trusted Him to provide, and He certainly has more than I could ever imagine. I cannot thank Him enough for blessing our business over the past few years and the wonderful customers we have.

I trust God that He will never leave me. If I fall or make a mistake, I look at it as a learning opportunity and what I can take away for the next time a situation like it occurs. I learned a lot about myself and others working in that toxic environment. Most importantly, if a job consistently steals my serenity and peace, it must go. No job is worth that.

HANDLING BAD DAYS

I used to think that sober people were superheroes. Now I know it is true. How do you not drink and handle bad days? I never thought about how to manage the bad days until they smacked me in the face. How do I know I am having a bad day? When I want to change the way I feel. I want to remove myself from the situation and disappear into a bottle of whatever I can get my hands on. Thankfully, God removed the obsession to drink a long time ago. I do not have a desire to drink any longer, but to change my mood.

I have been through divorce, family death, heartache, disappointment, job fails, friendship loss, and more, and I have not picked up a drink. I pull out my bag of recovery tools and work on doing exactly what I am supposed to when I have bad days. It is not always easy, and sometimes I have a meltdown before I reach for my tools, but I have used them each time where I needed them.

Here is what my friend wrote in one of my favorite books. She said, "If you can go through this list and do all of this and you still want to drink, then go for it." In no particular order:

- Go to a meeting and share what you are thinking.

- Call your sponsor.

- Call ten women and ask them how they are doing.

- Pray/Meditate.

- Work out.

- Read something about recovery.

- Listen to a speaker tape/podcast.

- Help someone or volunteer to be of service.

- Do random acts of kindness.

Guess what? I have never made it through even half of this list before I felt better. Some people say, "God willing, I will not have another drink." I say bull. God is totally willing for me to not drink. I am the one that makes the choice to not pick up and instead use my tools. Picking up is a choice.

FINDING MY PURPOSE

"I love when people who have been through hell walk out of the flames carrying buckets of water for those still consumed by the fire."

--Stephanie Sparkles

Let's get into the good stuff! The best part about recovery for me is helping others. I get to share my experience, plant a seed, and maybe help them in their life. What a gift I have to give others! Who knew?

Have you ever questioned what your purpose is in life? I did for as long as I can remember. I thought chasing a job title and a six-figure salary was what life was all about, and I was so wrong. Even with a title and the salary I desired, I was miserable. I felt empty going through life, knowing I had nothing to offer someone else other than a drinking friend or a sexually good time. What a lonely life and dark path that took me down. Thank you, Jesus, I am not that person anymore!

It was not until I was in the middle of working on myself that I realized my purpose was to serve others. That is what God wants all of us to do. "Do nothing out of selfish ambition or vain conceit. Rather, in humility value others above ourselves, not looking to your own interests but each of you to the interests of the others" (Philippians 2:3-4). I discovered my purpose working with women, not only those recovering from alcohol, but from other struggles as well.

I was told early in recovery, "You can't keep it unless you give it away." The *Alcoholics Anonymous* big book states, "Our very lives, as ex-problem drinkers, depend upon our constant thought of others and how we may help meet their needs." Every week I pray for God to show me who I can help and to send them to me. He sends me people through friends, the church, my job, and through social media. I constantly encourage and listen to others, and I get to share my experience and what Jesus did in my life.

There are many ways to serve others. Listening is an outstanding example of being there for someone else. People often do not share what is on their hearts or minds for fear of judgement. They bottle it up, which can lead to years of bondage. When I can give someone a safe place to open up about what they struggle with, it releases a little of that power the enemy has. The more you share and release, the weaker the enemy becomes until that struggle no longer rules your life. It does not have to be alcohol that is your stronghold. It can be anything that holds you back from freely living your life.

God changes us before He uses us. I had to change my heart and learn that my story is not meant to be kept a secret. Your struggle and how you healed and recovered is someone else's survival guide. Your story is unique, but there may be similarities with others, so look for them!

I did jail ministry for four years, and when the pandemic happened, I was not allowed to go in. I cannot wait to go back and serve because it is my favorite type of service work I have done to date. Every time I left there, I had this amazing feeling over me of pride and happiness. I never had that feeling being drunk or high on drugs. I know it is the Holy Spirit alive in me cheering me on for living out my purpose.

Going into a jail can feel intimidating and scary at first, but after a handful of times, I am confident I can reach women fairly quickly––at least the ones that are willing to receive what I share. There are always one or two women who are not ready to receive it, and that is okay. I still plant an idea for them. I like to qualify myself upfront and always share what I know will reach them by saying, "I am in recovery from alcohol and everything negative that is associated with it. I have been arrested and in jail several times. I am a survivor of sexual abuse, abandonment, and rejection from family. I have found a solution."

After attending church for about a year, I started my small group. I was already in a singles group, but it was hard to connect with others because no one could relate to what I went through, and I did not want to feel judged. The recovery meetings were great, but I wanted more—to learn and talk about Jesus with other women like myself. So, I started a group for women in recovery, whether it be addiction, abuse, divorce, trauma, PTSD, or anything that is a struggle, and I am blessed to do life with my soul sisters. I also joined a group like mine, led by Joyce, and started serving with her on a church greeter team. I wanted as many Jesus lovers around me as possible and found my tribe in these women.

God brings these women to me, and I facilitate the meetings. We do book studies on healing and areas we want to grow in and discuss how the teaching speaks to us and could help in our journey or life situation. We do sermon discussion and share our battles, prayer requests, and celebrate our praise reports.

If I lead the group, I usually start and share, then other women, and transformation happens in the group. When one of us opens up, it encourages another woman to speak up about her experience. We become vulnerable, authentic, and help carry each other through one another's struggles. It is the most beautiful intimacy to witness.

I have expressed many times that healing is a process from whatever stronghold you have in your heart and mind and can be extremely painful. However, the promise is on the other side of the pain. That promise is freedom. Freedom from chains, freedom from selfishness, and freedom from anger and resentment. My experience is the freedom comes from God, and Jesus is the answer!

It seemed taboo to talk about alcoholism and my sins at the beginning of my journey. It reveals a lot of negativity and stereotypes. Why would I talk about the harm I did to myself and others? I learned over time my story is not for me. It is to help or inspire someone else. I am not here to fix anyone but to share my life experience, and if you get something out of it, great. If not, that is okay, and God will bring the next person He wants me to help. I stole a phrase from my husband that I like to use. He is quite witty and the regular wise guy. *Some will, some won't. Who cares, who's next?*

I must remember that phrase when women come in and out of my small group like a revolving door. It is not for everyone, as I have had more than a hundred women sign up for the group. I used to take it personally when they did not come back after one or two meetings, and I felt hurt like I did something wrong. I learned some women are not willing to accept they have an issue, some are not ready to talk about it, some will not do the work it takes to get past it, some do not have the time, or it is not the right season. As long as there is a need for this type of group––which there is––I will continue to lead. The women that have stayed and done the work have made an amazing transformation, and that is why I love to lead the group. The best part is to see other women come into the group, do the work and grow, and then start their own group. What a miracle worker God is!

I encourage you to find a group that fits your needs if you are not in one already. Small groups are a part of my recovery formula, and I will continue because that is who I want to be around––women living in the solution and not in the problem. "For where two or three gather in my name, there I am with them" (Matthew 18:20).

Identifying Helpful Resources

There is no perfect formula out there for someone to heal and recover from whatever is holding them back from God's purpose. If there is a system, I have not found it. Nothing good comes easy, and recovery and healing is a hard challenge that can take years for some people. In my case, it has taken years and will continue. That is okay, because I am worth all the work I put into my growth and healing. I have found great value in living and being happy. I no longer want to hurt and wonder why.

I am eager to learn everything I can to be my best mentally, physically, and spiritually. You must take action to change, and that is where many people get stuck. Making excuses for not changing is easy to do. I did it far too long and could write a book on all the excuses I have made in my life. I knew I had an issue with alcohol twelve years before I finally stopped and made excuses almost daily.

There are so many resources available at your fingertips––just a quick google search away––to help with whatever struggle you have. There are hundreds of inspiring authors sharing stories of their experience and what works for them. If you are seeking help, there is hope. If you take one step each day towards your goal, that is progress!

There are many types of twelve-step programs that can help in your recovery journey, and they are not just for alcohol and drugs. I have attended or researched groups that include Alcoholics Anonymous (Al-anon), Adult Children of Alcoholics (ACA), Co-Dependents Anonymous (CoDA), and Celebrate Recovery (CR). In addition to my small group, I need to focus on one twelve-step program at a time because too much key principles and information can cause a meltdown for someone like me. Just know there are support groups out there for anything you need help with.

There are many self-help books on countless topics, and I cannot even tell you how many I have read over the years. Any book that was suggested to me, I read. I wish I had kept all the books because of my notes, but I gave a lot of them away. If God put it on my heart to give it to a woman I met along the way, I did. Today I keep my copy, and when I want to give someone a book, I get their address and go online and send it to them. I like to highlight and take notes in all my books and know I will want to reference them in the future or may revisit them in a book study with my small group.

Counseling came before I quit drinking and support groups after I quit. Since I have been sober, I continue to go back to counseling every time something new pops up or old resurfaces. I want to make sure I progress and heal in a healthy manner, and consistent guidance helps to keep myself in check. I want to be free and not in bondage anymore.

Getting honest with myself about my issues and sharing it with another person to receive feedback is where the power happened for me and continues to this day. When I feel myself off track, I typically call one of two people for a solution. As life unfolds with its challenges, I need to make sure I have resources and tools available at my fingertips. My number one go to is God. I learned early in my recovery journey from The *Alcoholics Anonymous* big book that says, "It is a daily reprieve based upon my spiritual condition." I must turn to God and surrender daily. In my case, I must sometimes surrender multiple times in the day. I strive to live in the solution today as much as possible. It might not seem like it some days, but I try my best.

I found a church home that I love. The messages I receive from the sermons always speak to me, and a lot of growth has resulted. God is always speaking to me through others because I am open to receive from Him. I am thirsty for knowledge and feel like I am just beginning on my long recovery journey. I started to read the Bible a couple of years ago and try to read daily to hear from God and learn.

I was a greeter at church with Joyce for a couple of years, then joined the care team to pray over people and connect them to life resources. A few years ago, I was not sure if I knew how to pray correctly, and instead of risking judgement by asking someone else, I googled "*how to pray.*" Praying over people was very scary at first, but I knew with practice I could grow to being good at it. After listening to others pray for years, I adopted parts I liked. Now I love the opportunity to pray for others.

Counseling is also part of my recovery formula. I have been in and out of counseling since I was court ordered at twenty-one from a DUI. I like to understand why I am how I am. When I connect with a professional and talk about a life issue or situation, they provide insight I did not think of before and help me with the solution. A counselor's perspective has been refreshing because mine was skewed or the worst-case scenario, and I have found a lot of healing from the anxiety, fear, and worry I had throughout my life.

Writing my story became part of my healing process, and I did not realize this until my book was almost complete. I was in the middle of writing when I discovered I had suppressed trauma that I never thought about. I did not believe the trauma was valid, and it was. My awareness happened when I was writing and then read it. I said out loud to Dave, "Oh my gosh, this is what I experienced during childhood. No wonder I became who I did. I had a traumatic childhood."

This realization was difficult to process at first. I never thought of it as trauma, just my life, so I never got professional help or talked about it. I went back to counseling, and my sessions were painful and filled with tears. Thankfully, healing came, and the stronghold was eventually lifted. I felt freedom yet again by surrendering to the process. God revealed to me, when the time was right, another opportunity to heal and grow. God's timing is always perfect. In the middle of the biggest challenges come the best triumphs.

I remember early in counseling talking often about my feelings of abandonment by my father. The counselor explained to me, "Him not being there for you has nothing to do with you as a person and not being good enough. It is about your father, his choices, and what is going on with him." Her insight made me feel better because at the time I just did not understand what I had done.

I have learned through counseling, recovery programs, and experience that alcoholics have many faces and cannot always be identified by a certain look. They are not just the homeless living under the bridge, which is what I thought at one time. Many alcoholics have families, careers, houses, go on vacations, and live full lives. They are as young as teenagers, and this disease affects every race and economic level. There are well-known celebrities and political faces in recovery. Alcoholism does not discriminate.

Addiction does not just hurt the person addicted but rips families apart, ruins lives, destroys relationships, ends careers, and affects anything in front of the drink or drug. It does not even have to run in your family genetics. I have met people in recovery who did not have addiction anywhere in their family lineage.

It is always nice to see when someone opens up on social media about their struggle, journey, or shares a sobriety birthday. This gives encouragement and hope to others. It is also very sad that perhaps a person you know has shared about losing a loved one to the fatal disease of addiction. You may have someone close whom you love that struggles with addiction. It is heartbreaking to understand it is everywhere and can happen to anyone.

GRATITUDE

Today I live in gratitude. Broken is a *choice*, and it is a choice that is never too late to make. I have great faith today because I have overcome where I have been, and God has delivered me from addiction and all the shame that came along with it. If you are in a broken place, there is a way to freedom. I knew I was an alcoholic for many years before I quit, but I was just in denial about it. I am very grateful my eyes were opened and that I decided to change. The pain, the unmanageability, and the emotional bankruptcy brought me to my knees in my closet when I wanted to kill myself, and I am grateful it made me who I am today. I wanted to live a little more than I wanted to die and was willing to do whatever it took to be someone else. I did not know what that looked like, but I trusted God could turn my train wreck of choices into something for good. He has done that beyond my expectations.

Recovery has been the greatest gift I never knew I wanted. I am grateful that I got honest with myself and realized that my life was powerless to alcohol and the poor choices that came along with the drinking and drugging. I am grateful that I was willing to get help and take suggestions from other people that had been down this road before. There is peace in my heart and mind, and I got a second chance at love. I am incredibly grateful to God for all He is doing in my life.

Gratitude was something that I had to take action with and often. My mindset dwelled on what I did not have for most of my life, and I sat in my misery and ruminated on negativity. I mentioned earlier in the book that I had a never satisfied mentality and was critical. I now focus on the abundant blessing of what I do have that truly matters, and this is the order of most importance to me:

- My relationship with God.

- My sobriety.

- My physical and mental health.

- My husband Dave.

- My business.

- My spiritual tribe.

If I do not have the top two daily, the truth is I will lose everything else. I am grateful for all the mornings I have woken up, thought of God first, and did not drink that day. God has turned my addictive patterns into something I can use for His purpose. I am grateful to God for all the good that has come into my life because I changed. It is occasionally a challenge to realize how blessed I am and at times feel like I do not deserve it or that they will go away. Dave reminds me, "Kelly, the blessings result from all the good choices you have made." If I continue to stay on the right path, God will take care of me. I know I will have bad days, but I can and will push through.

CLOSING

"Above all, be the heroine of your life, not the victim."
—Nora Ephron

FOR YOU

I pray God uses my experience, strength, and hope to bless you or someone you love. I pray that others can relate to the trauma and pain in my life. I pray that the mustard seed of hope that I held onto will bring strength and a first step to others. I pray that everything I learned that helped me will bless and encourage you on your life journey.

Testimonies encourage others in their faith, and I thought I had to be this perfect person to help someone else, but that is far from the truth. My long history of bad choices and turning it around is a beautiful testimony to show someone else that change is possible. Transformation happened because I surrendered to God and His will over my life. I chose not to stay broken.

Below are a few of my favorite scriptures on testimony. Someone shared their story with me many years ago, and when I was in despair and contemplating suicide, their experience gave me that small piece of hope that kept me alive.

"That is God working in us to take what the enemy meant for evil and turning it for good." (Genesis 50:20)

"God rescued us from dead-end alleys and dark dungeons. He has set us up in the kingdom of the Son he loves so much, the Son who got us out of the pit we were in, got rid of the sins we were doomed to keep repeating." (Colossians 1:13-14)

"We overcome by the blood of the Lamb and the word of our testimony. And they did not love their lives so much that they were afraid to die." (Revelation 12:11)

Every day I wake up and thank God for another day. I ask Him to show me someone that I can help and someone that can help me. God always puts people in my path daily to pray for, encourage, and serve.

Every person has a story about something they defeated, no matter how small it may seem. You never know how your experience could affect someone else looking to survive. I pray you do not hold on to it, but find the courage to share what happened and what worked for you to overcome it and find victory in your life.

I hope you found this book valuable and will share it with others. I would love to hear from you how it impacted your life or someone you know. God has a wonderful plan for each of our lives and patiently waits for us to take the first step towards Him. "For I know the plans I have for you" declares the Lord, "plans to prosper you and not to harm you, plans to give you hope and a future" (Jeremiah 29:11).

ABOUT THE AUTHOR

Kelly Staib is co-owner with her husband Dave of Freedom Pest Services LLC that operates in North and South Carolina. Kelly is a college graduate with a Bachelor of Science degree. In her spare time, she serves at church, leads a woman recovering life group, and leads recovery meetings in jails and institutions. When Kelly is not working and helping others, she likes to spend time on the lake, working out, and spending time with her tribe of women.

She is a bonus mom to Dave's two adult children Peyton and Logan. Kelly lives in Lake Wylie, SC, with her husband Dave and two dogs Hulk and Domino.